HEIRS OF SALVATION

Studies in biblical assurance

Heirs of Salvation

Studies in biblical assurance

D. Martyn Lloyd-Jones

BRYNTIRION PRESS

ISBN 1 85049 174 7

Unless otherwise stated, all Scripture quotations are from
the Authorised (King James) Version

Cover photograph: Phil Carden
Cover design: Phil Boorman @ burgum boorman ltd

Published by Bryntirion Press
Bryntirion Bridgend CF31 4DX, Wales, UK
Printed by Creative Print & Design, Ebbw Vale

Contents

Blessèd assurance, Jesus is mine:
  O what a foretaste of glory divine!
Heir of salvation, purchase of God,
  Born of His Spirit, washed in His blood.
Frances Jane Van Alstyne

1
Abel:
assured worship

'But as many as received him, to them gave he power to become the sons of God, even to them that believe on his name: which were born, not of blood, nor of the will of the flesh, nor of the will of man, but of God.'
(John 1:12-13)

'By faith Abel offered unto God a more excellent sacrifice than Cain, by which he obtained witness that he was righteous, God testifying of his gifts: and by it he being dead yet speaketh.'
(Hebrews 11:4)

In verses 12 and 13 of the first chapter of John's Gospel we are reminded that the ultimate end and object of salvation is not merely that we should be forgiven, but that we who believe on the Lord Jesus Christ should become the children of God. That is what all who believe in Christ are destined unto. That is why the Word was made flesh and dwelt among us; that is why he lived and died and rose again.

Now this is the most wonderful message that we can ever hear. There is nothing that is in any way comparable to this amazing fact that we can be made 'the children of God: and if children, then heirs; heirs of God, and joint-heirs with Christ' (Romans 8:16-17). This is the teaching of the New Testament and nothing is more important than that we should know it. Christians are

7

meant to know that they are the children of God; they are meant to rejoice in this knowledge; they are meant to be happy, blessed, in the true sense of the word.

Now two types of assurance are offered to us. First, there is the assurance that comes *by deduction from the Scriptures*. We receive this type of assurance in two ways. The first way is by believing the plain statements of Scripture. For example, we read the promise that says, 'He that believeth on him is not condemned' (John 3:18), and know that if we believe we are not condemned. The second way is by testing ourselves against what we are told in the Scriptures is always true of Christians.

But secondly, over and above that, assurance comes *by the direct witness of the Spirit*: 'The Spirit itself beareth witness with our spirit, that we are the children of God' (Romans 8:16).

But how can we obtain this second type of assurance? What do we have to do in order to have the knowledge that we are indeed the children of God and are well pleasing in his sight? It seems to me that perhaps the best way to approach this question is to look at some examples of men and women who, like ourselves, have been in this world of time but who nevertheless have rejoiced in this assurance. So I propose to consider some of the people who are put before us in the eleventh chapter of Hebrews.

A gallery of portraits

First, let me remind you of the words that introduce the 'gallery of portraits' that we have here: 'Now faith is the substance of things hoped for, the evidence of things not seen. For by it the elders obtained a good report. Through faith we understand that the worlds were framed by the word of God, so that things which are seen were not made of things which do appear' (Hebrews 11:1-3). And then the writer turns to his first illustration, which is the case of Abel: 'By faith Abel offered unto God a more excellent sacrifice than Cain' (v.4).

The author of Hebrews was writing to some very discouraged Christian people. They had been brought up as Jews, but had heard the preaching of the gospel and had believed it. Now, however, many were doubting and uncertain. Many were looking back to their old religion with longing eyes, and were in a state of what we nowadays call defeatism. The result was that they were thoroughly depressed. We can say that their trouble was that they were lacking assurance of salvation.

The author's whole object in writing was to give his readers the assurance they needed. He has given profound doctrine concerning the Lord Jesus Christ and his work. He has been arguing it out, he has been exhorting his readers on the basis of it, and he has been issuing terrible warnings. And now, having done all that, in order to help and encourage them, he says in effect, 'Look here, all your troubles and your difficulties are nothing new. God's people have always had a hard time in this world, and yet in spite of that they have gone on and have triumphed. What was their secret?' Then he gives this list of their great forebears, and points out that they all prevailed because each one lived a life of faith, or, to use his words, they went through this world 'by faith'.

Having given his list, the writer says, 'Wherefore seeing we also are compassed about with so great a cloud of witnesses, let us lay aside every weight, and the sin which doth so easily beset us, and let us run with patience the race that is set before us' (Hebrews 12:1). So in this eleventh chapter he is giving examples of men and women who triumphed because they knew that they were the children of God. They knew that all was well with their souls because they were sure of their relationship to their heavenly Father.

Now I propose to follow exactly the same method as the writer of this epistle. I trust that nobody is surprised that I am going back to these Old Testament characters. If you have any difficulty about that you should ask yourself this question: Why did the author of this epistle do that? After all, he was writing to Christians, and

9

they were as much Christians as we are; yet he put before them these Old Testament saints. And his reason is perfectly simple. God remains the same, and the children of Israel, the true children of Israel, were as much the children of God as we are, as the fourth chapter of Galatians reminds us.

We who are Christians are children of faith, and we are therefore children of Abraham. The great message of the New Testament is that the Gentiles have been made 'fellow-heirs' with the Jews (Ephesians 3:6). We have been added, we have been brought in, to the same kingdom. That is what causes Paul to glory so much in Ephesians 2 and 3.

So there need be no problem about this. The relationship of the believer to God is essentially the same in both the Old Testament and the New. Abraham was a child of God, so was Abel, so were all these men and women. The difference is that in the Old Testament dispensation this relationship expressed itself primarily in a material and external manner, whereas now it is mainly a matter of spiritual relationships and conditions, something that is unseen.

The only other difference is that you and I, looking back as we do upon the finished work of Christ—whereas they looked forward to it—should have a much greater assurance than these Old Testament saints ever had. They simply saw these things 'afar off', as the author of Hebrews puts it (Hebrews 11:13). 'These all, having obtained a good report through faith, received not the promises: God having provided some better thing for us, that they without us should not be made perfect' (Hebrews 11:39-40). So as we look at these people we must say to ourselves, 'Well, that's the minimum of what I ought to have. I should have much more, because I'm in a superior position.'

'A good report'

So let us look at these men and women. We are told that they 'obtained a good report' (v.39). Now that expression, 'a good report', is also used in the fourth verse, where we read: 'by which he *obtained witness* that he was righteous'. These people obtained 'witness' that they were good, that they were righteous in the sight of God.

In other words, the writer is telling us that God let all these Old Testament saints know that he was pleased with them, that they were his people, and that, whatever the world might do to them, he was preparing a place for them and they were going to enter it for certain. So they are great illustrations of people with an assurance of salvation, people with an absolute certainty, though they were still living in this world of time and were encompassed about with all sorts of difficulties, trials and weaknesses.

Now as we come to look at these men and women we shall find that one thing is common to them all, and that is, as the author puts it, that they walked 'by faith'. 'Faith is the substance'—the substantiating, the guaranteeing—'of things hoped for, the evidence of things not seen.' It is faith, he says, that gives assurance.

And yet we shall see that we are not merely given a list of people who all show exactly the same characteristics. There are differences between them which are extremely valuable to us because, though we are all Christians, we are not all identical. There are variations in our personalities, even as there were in the personalities of these people. There are variations in the things that happen to us, and the times in which we live. All these factors make a difference. But we find these people in their varying circumstances still possessing the same assurance and still living the same fundamental life of faith.

And so if we want to know something about how to get assurance, if we are lacking in it, nothing is more profitable than to observe these people, to see what their secret was. What brought them to this position of assurance? 'God testifying of his gifts', we are told about Abel (v.4). It is the same in the case of Enoch: 'Enoch was translated that he should not see death; and was not found, because God had translated him: for before his translation he had this testimony, that he pleased God' (v.5). God testified to every one of them. That is the basic and fundamental factor. God lets his people know that they are his people and that he is well pleased with them.

So that is our theme, and the question for every one of us is this: Do we know that we are the children of God? Has God given us the witness and the testimony that he is well pleased with us, that we are his people? Every one of these people had this assurance, and every one of us is meant to have it. Christians are not meant to be uncertain about their salvation. Christians are not merely men and women who hope to be saved. They know it. They should be rejoicing in their salvation and living a life of triumph in this world of time.

Cain and Abel

So we come to our first example, and it is particularly interesting, even if for no other reason than that Abel is the earliest illustration of the life of faith. Here is the first man of whom we are told that God let him know that he was well pleased with him. The first example is always important, and for his first illustration the author of Hebrews very rightly goes back to the very beginning.

But there is another great advantage about this first illustration, and that is that the truth is put to us in the form of a contrast. In most of the other examples we are given the man himself, but here we are given the man in contrast with another—his brother Cain. We are always helped, are we not, by a negative? You see the thing itself and then you see it by contrast, and sometimes it is easier to see a thing by contrast than it is to see it directly. If you look at a thing directly, you think you have understood it, but then you see the opposite, the contrast, and the lineaments of the first stand out more prominently and clearly.

Here, then, we have before us Cain and Abel. Abel is the man who pleased God, while Cain did not. So we must concentrate our attention upon Abel in particular, and see what it was about him that made him the man he was, what it was that gave him the blessed assurance that this author is so anxious for the Hebrew Christians to have, and that every one of us should possess.

Two types of worshipper

The picture we have here is of two men worshipping God. Cain was as much a worshipper as Abel. We have a picture of two men presenting an offering to God just as two people may enter any church. So the mere fact that we are found in a place of worship, in the posture of worship, is not sufficient, in and of itself, to please God.

The major lesson that comes out here is the contrast between the two men. This is remarkable because they were brothers, children of the same parents. They had been brought up in the same home; they had lived in the same atmosphere; they had been subjected to the same teaching. They had everything in common. Yet there was a fundamental difference and cleavage.

And here, at the dawn of history, we see a perfect summary of the story of the human race. The whole of humanity is either Cain or Abel. This is true in the Church as well as outside. And here, at the very beginning, God has presented us with this great illustration in order that we may learn a profound and fundamental lesson. Why is it possible for us to be Christians and not know it? Why is it possible for people to think that they are Christians without being Christians? Why is it unfortunately not true to say that because we are members of churches we are therefore Christians? Well, here is the answer, and here also is the key to the whole secret of how we can be certain that we are truly Christian, and have assurance and rejoice in it.

13

Now Cain and Abel are the first of a great series that runs through the Old Testament. After Cain and Abel we read of Isaac and Ishmael, both sons of Abraham, and yet what different men they were! Then comes the notorious case of Jacob and Esau. Twins. The same father and mother, in the womb together, born, as it were, at exactly the same moment, and yet what a fundamental difference!

And so it continues. We see Sarah and Hagar, and then, later on, the false prophets and the true prophets of Israel. They were all prophets, they were all holding the same office, and they all addressed the same people in the same circumstances: but some were true prophets and some were false.

And within the children of Israel themselves there was a fundamental cleavage, so that the apostle Paul was able to say, 'For they are not all Israel, which are of Israel' (Romans 9:6). Someone could be a member of the nation of Israel and yet not be a true Israelite. Running through the whole of the Old Testament is this division between Abel and Cain, the true and the false.

And, of course, in the New Testament, we find exactly the same thing. Even in the pages of the four Gospels we see the true and the false worshipper. Our Lord painted it for us in his parable of the tax collector and the Pharisee, who both went up into the temple to pray. There are two men in the same temple, both going to pray and worship God, yet our Lord says that only one returns to his house blessed and justified. Here is the very thing we are concerned about. The mere fact that we are in God's house does not tell us anything; the false can be present as well as the true. How can we be certain that we are the true? How can we know that we are pleasing in God's sight?

Notice how the apostle Paul puts the same contrast in Galatians 4. He says that there are always two Jerusalems, the Jerusalem that is above and that which is on the earth. There is always, he says, a perpetuation of this antagonism, this difference

14

between Hagar and Sarah. The false is always opposed to the true. He might very well have said that Cain is always opposing Abel.

And the same split runs right through the subsequent history of the Christian Church. There has always been a division between the apparently Christian and the truly Christian, those who know that they are the children of God, and those who do not. They are absolutely different, though on the surface they may appear to be identical.

Two approaches to worship

Then our second principle is found when we ask this question: What are the causes of the difference? And this one illustration of Cain and Abel gives us the key. It is as we look at the differences between these two men that we find the whole secret of how to be well pleasing in God's sight, how to get this testimony, this witness, that God is our Father and that he is pleased with us, a testimony that God gives to his own people and to nobody else.

So let us observe the differences. They are to be seen in Cain and Abel's approaches to worship, which can be subdivided under three headings.

A different view of authority

The first is a different view of authority. I may want to worship God; both Abel and Cain desired to worship God; but how does one worship him? And the moment you ask that question, you see the first difference. In the last analysis, there are only two ways of worshipping God: either through self, or by faith. 'By faith Abel offered unto God a more excellent sacrifice than Cain' (v.4). Abel worshipped God by faith; Cain did not. So what was it that guided Cain? Well, there is no difficulty about this. Cain himself decided what he was going to do. The contrast is between a man acting on faith and a man acting on his own reason, his own understanding, his own opinion.

15

Now this word 'faith', of course, is important; it is the key to everything—'By faith Abel . . .' And this simply means that he acted according to the instructions that had been given. There is no doubt at all but that these two brothers had received teaching from their father and mother, who in turn had been instructed by God. So they were both confronted by the same teaching, and we are told here that whereas Abel believed the teaching and acted upon it, approaching God in the way that the teaching had instructed him, Cain did not. Abel, you see, presented an animal sacrifice, whereas Cain took the fruit of the ground, the crops that he himself had produced. There was no animal, there was no blood, there was no sacrifice. That is the difference, and it is a difference between obedience and disobedience to the teaching.

This principle is as true today as it has ever been. The whole purpose of the Bible is to instruct us in the way to approach God and worship him. The Bible gives God's teaching on how he is to be found, how he is to be worshipped, and what is well pleasing in his sight. This teaching is perfectly plain; he has put it before us, even as he put it before Abel and Cain.

So the first secret is that men and women who are well pleasing in God's sight obey him. They do not act according to their own ideas. Every one of us, in our approach to God and to the question of religion, is in one of two positions. We either believe the Bible to be the Word of God and submit ourselves completely to its teaching, or else we take it upon ourselves, by our own reason and understanding and knowledge, to decide what is right.

Now Cain obviously took the second course. In effect, he said, 'Yes, I do want to worship God, I want to acknowledge his goodness, and I think this is the way to do it.' So he presented some of the fruit of the ground to God. It may have been quite a good offering, we do not know, but we do know that it was not what was commanded. He did not act according to faith; he did not submit himself to the revelation that had been given.

Now this is so vital that I must pause with it for a moment. You will never have true assurance of salvation unless you worship God in the way that he has indicated. The first secret of assurance is submission to God's revelation. Some people say, 'Of course, nowadays we no longer believe what the apostle Paul said, he was only a man of his day. Even Jesus Christ was a child of his age. What did he know? We know so much more.' But if you say that, you will never have assurance of salvation—never. If you think that you know more than the Bible knows about how God is to be approached and worshipped, you are already putting yourself out, you belong to Cain and not to Abel.

We do not speculate as to what God is like. We do not begin to say, 'He is not "up there" or "out there", he is depth.' We do not bring our own philosophical ideas about God. No, we start by saying, 'We know nothing about God and we cannot examine him because God is infinite and everlasting and eternal. We know nothing about God except that which he himself has revealed to us in the Bible, and we submit completely to that.' That is the beginning of faith.

A different spirit

Secondly, when Cain and Abel worshipped God, there was a difference in their spirits. Now, in the case of Cain, it is quite clear that worship was a formal matter. He wanted to acknowledge God in general and to render up his thanks for the benefits that he had received. But he does not seem to have gone any further. He said, 'Very well, I've got good crops, I've been successful, and I'll acknowledge this to God.'

But it was a formality. There was no faith involved. And there are many people who worship God like that. There are many people, even now, in days like these, who believe in attending

17

formal acts of public worship, but think that is all they need to do. They have shown respect to God, they have taken an external action, and there it is, finished with. Then they go on and live their own lives in their own ways and you would never imagine that they were Christians at all, and indeed, they probably are not; they are formal worshippers. Cain takes his offering; these people go to a place of worship once on a Sunday, or perhaps only once a year. Now and again they may go to a thanksgiving service, a harvest thanksgiving, or some other thanksgiving, even as Cain did. They take the fruit of the ground, and feel they have done very well because they have acknowledged God.

I know many people who still say their prayers even though they deny the whole of the Christian faith. 'I've always believed in God and I've never failed to say my prayers', they say. 'I like to listen to an occasional sermon. I might read a religious book.' They acknowledge God. But it is entirely formal and external. The heart is not in it; the spirit is not involved; there is no rejoicing, no thoroughness. And they know nothing about assurance of salvation, or the blessings of salvation.

But Abel took the best he could offer. Abel's heart and spirit were involved. He did not give his own labour but a living sacrifice, as it were. The whole spirit of the worship, and the approach, were entirely different.

A different understanding
But thirdly, and most important of all, Cain and Abel had a different understanding of what God wanted. 'By faith Abel offered unto God a more excellent sacrifice than Cain.' Why? Because he understood the teaching. Why was it that Abel took this animal, killed it and offered the blood? What made him do it? Was it his own idea? No, no, it was 'by faith' that he did it, and faith means 'response to the revelation'. That is the meaning of faith in the whole of the Bible from beginning to end. The men and women of

18

faith are those who have believed God; that was the secret of every one of them. Abel was the first. He believed the teaching and he acted upon it.

What was the teaching? There can be no difficulty about this. It was that in worshipping God, in approaching him, we must have a sacrifice, a life must be laid down; and the sacrifice must be a blood sacrifice since the life is in the blood. We find hints of this teaching in Genesis chapter 3. After Adam and Eve had fallen, God spoke to them in the Garden and gave them a great promise. He said he would put enmity between the seed of the woman and the seed of the serpent. And the seed of the woman would bruise the serpent's head, but in doing so, his heel would be bruised (see Genesis 3:15).

The Lord Jesus Christ is 'the seed of the woman' and that is the first prophecy concerning his death on Calvary's hill. He would conquer, yes, but he would be bruised, he would be wounded. It would cost him; it would involve suffering; there would be shedding of blood. There it is at the very beginning.

There are those who see the institution of sacrifice even in the coats of skin that God made to clothe Adam and Eve. There they were in their nakedness, and God clothed them with the skins of animals. The clothing was the result of a death, of the shedding of blood. In other words, the righteousness of Christ is prefigured. We are only clothed with his righteousness after he has died for us. There is the adumbration of the teaching.

And what is so obvious is that Abel had believed the teaching, while Cain had not. Cain said: 'I'm going to worship God. I've done well. I'll take the best of my crop, the fruit that I've grown myself, which is the result of my work. I'll present that to God and God will be pleased with it and all will be well.'

But Abel said: 'No, no. That's not enough. We are sinners and our best is unworthy in the presence of God. All our righteousness is as filthy rags. God has told us that he will not accept it. Sin must be punished, and the punishment is death. God prefigures

19

that he is going to send one who will die for us, and we are to remember this as we approach him. He instructs us to take an animal, put our hands upon it, transfer our sins to it, slay it and take the blood and offer it to God. That is the way.'

In other words, Abel went into the presence of God conscious of the fact that he was a sinner. He went into the presence of God acknowledging his sin and his guilt, his shame and his utter need. He acknowledged that he was entirely dependent upon the mercy of God. He was like the tax collector who said, 'God be merciful to me a sinner' (Luke 18:13). Cain, on the other hand, went in with self-righteousness and self-confidence, giving what *he* could offer, what *he* had produced, feeling that his works were acceptable before God. Immediately we see the cleavage.

Now these things are tremendously important. The author of Hebrews puts the case of Abel and Cain before us in connection with this whole matter of assurance. Abel was given assurance: Cain was not. And in their approaches to worship you have the secret of it all.

Do you submit yourself utterly to God's revelation and his way of salvation? Do you come before God like the Pharisee, thanking him that you are not like other people? Do you feel that you are paying God a compliment when you enter his house? Are you relying upon your act of worship, your formal acknowledgement of God? It is useless! It is utterly rejected!

There is only one way to approach God in worship, and that is as a vile sinner, recognising your utter sinfulness and condemnation, and looking only unto, and relying solely upon, the Lord Jesus Christ and his laying down his life upon the cross on Calvary's hill for you and for your sins. 'Without shedding of blood [there] is no remission [of sins]' (Hebrews 9:22). There is only one way into the presence of God, there is only one way through which we can go with boldness into the Holiest of All, and that, as the writer has already put it in verse 19 of chapter 10, is 'by the blood of Jesus'—the way Abel went. And without this there is no hope whatsoever of assurance. At the very dawn of history this matter has been laid down once and for ever.

Two receptions

But let me end by showing you the different receptions that were given to the two types of worshipper.

Cain and his offering

Cain, I have no doubt, thought that he was doing very well. He was very pleased with himself when he took his offering. That is always the tragedy about the false professor, the false worshipper: he is pleased with himself, like the Pharisee. Look again at our Lord's picture: 'God, I thank thee, that I am not as other men are . . . or even as this publican. I fast twice in the week, I give tithes of all that I possess' (Luke 18:11-12). Self-satisfied, self-contained, very pleased with himself and with his formal act of worship, he went right to the front and there he congratulated himself.

False worshippers persuade themselves for a while that their offerings are accepted by God, but they never know real assurance. God never tells such people that he is well pleased with them—they tell God that they are pleased with themselves.

And yet we must have the testimony of God to the fact that we are accepted. What we need is the Spirit bearing witness with our spirits that we are the children of God. I can persuade myself that I am this and that, but it does not satisfy me, I want an 'assurance clear' from God. That is what we need: God testifying with us that we are his children. Cain never had it. The Pharisee never had it. The false believer never has it. People who trust to their own acts of worship never have it, they never can.

But we must go even beyond that. God not only does not tell such people that he is pleased with them; ultimately, he tells them that he is not pleased with them, and this is the terrible thing. It is

21

brought out in a dramatic manner in this old story. We are told: 'The LORD had respect unto Abel and to his offering: but unto Cain and to his offering he had not respect. And Cain was very wroth, and his countenance fell' (Genesis 4:4-5).

This is the terrible thing about false worship, about a pseudo-Christianity. It may think that all is well for the time being, and it may keep itself going on that, but as certainly as we are alive, God dislikes it, he is not pleased with it, and he always makes that known. He may delay showing his disapproval, some time may pass, but he always does make it known. The happiness of the false is short-lived; it soon comes to an end, and it is a terrible end when it does come.

Cain realised it. We are told that 'his countenance fell' and he was filled with anger. He said, as it were: 'Look what I've done! Look at the offering I've presented! What's the matter with God? Why doesn't he bless me?' Antagonism to God! His spirit was always wrong. He never knew God. He was only pleasing himself. And here he is, in misery, and even worse will follow.

I repeat that God is not only not pleased with such an act of worship; he is *displeased* with it, and he always shows his displeasure. Do you remember our Lord's terrifying words about those people who at the end will say, 'Lord, Lord, have we not prophesied in thy name? and in thy name have cast out devils? and in thy name done many wonderful works?' Our Lord said, 'Then will I profess unto them, I never knew you: depart from me, ye that work iniquity' (Matthew 7:22-23).

These people were pleased with their works. They said that they were doing them for his name. They were saying, 'Lord, Lord.' But he said, 'I have never known you. I have nothing to do with you.' They had never had assurance, and now they know that they are cast out and destroyed.

Or take the case of the five foolish virgins. They are professing believers who want to be at the bridal party. Yet when they hammer at the door, it is not opened. They are outside, and they remain outside. Here is the terrible lesson running through the whole Bible. The Cain type never has true assurance and always ends in suffering and shame and despair.

Abel and his offering

God shows his pleasure to those who are true. '[Abel] obtained witness that he was righteous, God testifying of his gifts.' How did God do that? It really does not matter. There are those who believe that the fire of God descended upon the offering on the altar. It may or may not have done. All I know is that the principle taught in the whole Bible is that if your offering is true, God will let you know. If you come in the right way, God will give you some heart-satisfaction. There will be a genuine peace, and you will know that it is from God. God will always bear you witness. God will always testify that your gift is acceptable. Any man or woman who pleads the blood of Christ with a penitent heart is always given some sort of assurance.

But that does not of necessity mean that you will have an easy time of it. Remember what happened to Abel! The moment Abel did the right thing, his brother became jealous and envious. Cain persecuted Abel and finally he killed him. So this is rather a wonderful test as to whether or not we are Christians. If people tell you that you are taking your Christianity too seriously, you have very good evidence that you are a Christian. If the formal religious person tells you that you are going a little bit mad and that you are suffering from a religious complex, thank him for it. He is giving proof that you are Abel and that he is Cain. If people say, 'All you need to do is live a good life—what are you talking about the blood for?' then you are Abel and they are Cain. Right through the Bible the true professor has been persecuted and hated by the false.

As long as you are a formal worshipper, you will never have any persecution. But once you become a true professor, once you

23

get a knowledge of Christ in your heart, once you become a real child of God, you will find that others will show their teeth. They will hate you; they will condemn you; they will try somehow or another to destroy you. They may even do what Cain did to Abel—it has often happened in the history of the Church. It is the Church, the formal professor, that has persecuted the true Christian, even unto death. This is a terrifying thing, but it is true; this is Church history.

So I am not here to say that if you present your true offering to God in the right way, then you will never have any problems. These people described in Hebrews chapter 11 had terrible troubles, and yet they triumphed. Why? Because they knew that they were God's children. They said:

> *Man may trouble and distress me,*
> *'Twill but drive me to Thy breast.*
> Henry Francis Lyte

> *When peace like a river attendeth my way,*
> *When sorrows like sea billows roll;*
> *Whatever my lot, Thou hast taught me to say,*
> *It is well, it is well with my soul.*
> Horatio Gates Spafford

Nothing matters but this. If you know you are a child of God, if he gives you the testimony, then, though hell be let loose, though everything go against you, you will be able to turn to him and say, '"Thy lovingkindness is better than life." Let them kill me, let them do what they like with me, nothing can rob me of the knowledge that I am your child and that I am going on to enjoy my eternity with you.'

Oh, says our Lord to these disciples as he sends them out, 'Fear not them which kill the body, but are not able to kill the soul: but rather fear him which is able to destroy both soul and body in hell' (Matthew 10:28).

No, no, we are not promised an easy time, but if you come as Abel came, God will tell you that he is well pleased. Let the whole world laugh at you and deride you and mock you and persecute you and try to kill you; it does not matter; he will tell you that you belong to him, that you are his dear child, and that he will never leave you nor forsake you. That is the message: 'he being dead yet speaketh'.

So I leave you with a question: Has Abel spoken to you? Is Abel still speaking to you? Is he telling you that there is only one way to find true acceptance with God, only one way whereby you can have a real and a lasting assurance, and that is by submission to the revelation, with a true spirit, an honest, open heart, and an utter, absolute dependence upon Jesus Christ and him crucified? 'The blood of Jesus Christ his Son cleanseth us from all sin' (1 John 1:7).

That is the message of Abel to us. Have we heard it? Have we learned it? Merely to present ourselves is not enough. Merely to take the posture of worship is not enough. There is only one way into the Holiest of All: it is by the blood of Jesus. If you acknowledge that, God will acknowledge you and give you the testimony that you are his child and that you are well pleasing in his sight.

2
Enoch:
walking with God

*'But as many as received him, to them gave he power
to become the sons of God, even to them that believe on his
name: which were born, not of blood, nor of the will of the flesh,
nor of the will of man, but of God.'*
(John 1:12-13)

*'By faith Enoch was translated that he should not see death;
and was not found, because God had translated him: for
before his translation he had this testimony, that he pleased
God. But without faith it is impossible to please him:
for he that cometh to God must believe that he is, and that
he is a rewarder of them that diligently seek him.'*
(Hebrews 11:5-6)

Our basic theme, let me remind you, is that there is nothing more important for us in this world than to know that we are the children of God. This is true for two main reasons: first, we cannot enjoy the Christian life unless we have this assurance; second, and much more important, we cannot function truly as the children of God unless we are clear about our title deeds, unless we know who we are.

We live in an evil world, and your business and mine is to show the world a better way—the way of God. Our responsibility, therefore, is very great. We must not only look at our own state and condition, but we must be settled about it so that we can

27

represent God and the Lord Jesus Christ to the world that is round and about us. The apostle Paul says in his letter to the Philippians that Christians 'shine as lights in the world; holding forth the word of life' (Philippians 2:15-16). They are 'sons of God, without rebuke, in the midst of a crooked and perverse generation' (Philippians 2:15)—a true description of Christians at this present time.

Now we are not simply to denounce the crookedness, but to 'shine forth as lights', as luminaries in the heavens, showing a better, a more glorious way. And the first step towards fulfilling that task is to be certain that we are the children of God. Christians who are uncertain are of no value. They do not represent God and the Lord Jesus Christ. They have to spend all their time looking at themselves, thinking about themselves, wanting some help for themselves, instead of being concerned about their responsibility to the world that is outside.

So we must be absolutely certain, and that is why we are now looking at some examples from Hebrews 11 of men and women like ourselves, in this same world, battling with the same, or oftentimes worse, conditions, who nevertheless lived triumphantly and gloriously, and bore their witness to the truth of the things of God. They won through, the writer tells us, by faith, and in exactly the same way we must succeed by faith.

Furthermore, the thing that the writer emphasises about them all is this: 'By it [by faith] the elders obtained a good report' (v.2); witness was borne unto them that God was well pleased with them. That, he says, is the secret of every one of them.

We have already examined this in the case of Abel, and now we look at Enoch. I have already indicated that we must not think that every one of these cases is identical with all the others. Fundamentally, of course, they are the same; we are looking at men and women of faith, but in each instance some particular aspect or angle of faith is brought out. As we come, therefore, to

28

look at Enoch, we shall find that something is taught us here which was not taught with the same fullness in the case of Abel.

'By faith Enoch . . .'

Now there are three main references to Enoch in the Bible, and if we are to learn the lesson truly, it is very important that we should be clear about the historical details that we are given. The first reference to Enoch is in Genesis 5:

And Enoch lived sixty and five years, and begat Methuselah: and Enoch walked with God after he begat Methuselah three hundred years, and begat sons and daughters: and all the days of Enoch were three hundred sixty and five years: and Enoch walked with God: and he was not; for God took him (verses 21-24).

Then there is the reference here in Hebrews 11:5-6, and a further reference comes in the Epistle of Jude, verses 14 and 15, where we read:

And Enoch also, the seventh from Adam, prophesied of these [of the evil that was to come, that is like the 'raging waves of the sea, foaming out their own shame'] saying, Behold, the Lord cometh with ten thousands of his saints, to execute judgment upon all, and to convince all that are ungodly among them of all their ungodly deeds which they have ungodly committed, and of all their hard speeches which ungodly sinners have spoken against him.

Here, surely, is a most important case, and we see how up to date the Scriptures are.

Do not forget that Enoch lived in those terrible, horrible days before the Flood, those awful, dissolute, sinful days that are described in the sixth chapter of Genesis. He lived in that age that led to the judgement of the Flood, when men and women gave themselves to sin and vice of every description.

Yet we are told that Enoch lived and walked with God and was well pleasing in God's sight, so much so that he was translated into heaven without experiencing natural, physical death. He is one of two men who did not die in the usual manner, the other being the prophet Elijah. The bodies of both men were changed in some manner that we cannot understand, and they were taken just as they were immediately into heaven and the presence of God.

That subject does not concern us now, but it is, of course, notable and remarkable. And, incidentally, it shows us the importance of the doctrine of the resurrection of the body, a doctrine that we must never surrender. After death, we do not merely go on as spirits, but the whole person is saved. The body is to be redeemed as well as the soul and spirit.

Now the important fact about Enoch, as the writer of Hebrews reminds us, is that 'before his translation he had this testimony, that he pleased God' (v.5). That is the reason why he was spared the agony and the suffering of death and all that is involved in the dissolution of the body. That was the secret of this man Enoch.

Now that, I emphasise again, is the common factor in the lives of all these people who are mentioned in Hebrews 11. They were given the knowledge, the certain knowledge, that they were well pleasing to God; they were given a 'testimony'. You remember how Abel was given to know that God was pleased with his gift. He was not uncertain, but was given assurance. Before he was murdered by his brother he was rejoicing in the certainty of his relationship to God.

Enoch is the writer's second example of a man who enjoyed full assurance of salvation. The importance of that for us is this: it was because he enjoyed this assurance that Enoch was able to live as he did in his day and generation. Amidst the sin and the

30

vice and the evil of that pre-deluge world this man stood out as a light in the heavens. He rejoiced in his relationship to God, and he was a rebuke to all the ungodliness that was rampant round and about him.

The 'testimony'

The first thing that arises for our consideration is therefore this: How exactly was Enoch given this testimony that he pleased God?

Incidentally, at this point I would entirely disagree with the interpretation given by the great Dr John Owen, who says that the testimony is the testimony that is given of Enoch in the Scriptures. But the Scriptures tell us that the testimony was given *before* his translation, and the Scriptures were not written until some considerable period of time afterwards. No, no, this testimony is not the mere record of Enoch in the Scriptures. He was given it, as all these men were given it. It was personal, subjective; it was in the realm of assurance of salvation.

So how was Enoch given this testimony that he pleased God? Well, I have no hesitation in saying that the answer is found in the description given of him in Genesis 5:24—'And Enoch walked with God.' Now I shall show you later that these words refer to the way, the manner, in which Enoch lived. But there is something much more important, and it is this: Enoch *knew* that he was walking with God. God gave Enoch the privilege of his companionship. Enoch knew that he was walking in the presence of God. He knew God—God was his companion. And God made it quite clear to Enoch that he loved him, that he was well pleased with him, and that he was a man after his own heart.

Now we are told about Abraham that he was 'the friend of God' (2 Chronicles 20:7; James 2:23). That, together with walking with God, is over and above believing in God. The picture is of two companions walking along a road together, each one conscious of the presence of the other. And I am suggesting that God made it clear to Enoch that he was well pleased with him by letting him know that he was with him, by giving him intimations of his nearness, by speaking to him and blessing him in different ways, giving him an intimate, personal realisation that he was there.

Let me quote the statement of an old Puritan called Bolton, who lived in the seventeenth century. He quotes a man who left this as his message to men and women: 'God dealeth familiarly with men.' And he does. We find many instances in the Old Testament. That is the story of the patriarchs. God came down, as it were, and spoke to them. They knew. They had a direct, immediate knowledge, which is the height of assurance, as we have already seen, and Enoch is a perfect instance of that. 'Enoch walked with God.' Over and above his faith he had absolute certainty. As God gave certainty to Jacob, enabling him to say, 'This is none other but the house of God, and this is the gate of heaven' (Genesis 28:17)—God is here—so he gave it to Enoch, possibly in a much more striking manner.

The question we ask ourselves, therefore, is this: Do we know anything about that? Do we know anything about walking with God? Do we know anything of God giving us his testimony that he is well pleased with us? Has he given us these intimations? This is what is important. Without it, we cannot function truly as Christians in this evil hour.

Now you notice my argument. I am not here to denounce people who are not Christians. That is a very simple and easy thing to do. But that is not the ultimate business of the Church. Mere denunciation of evil is obvious; it is easy; it is cheap. A great deal of that takes place, but it is of value to nobody. The Church must show this other way. What the world needs to know is that it is possible for a man or woman to walk with God even in this evil world. That is what we must look for. We can feel very happy as we say,

32

'Thank God, I'm not like that man!' But that is sheer pharisaism. The question for you is not 'Are you unlike that man?' but 'Are you like Enoch?' The need of the hour is a church filled with men and women like Enoch, who walk with God! That is the way to reform the Church and the world, and any concentration on negatives alone will get us nowhere.

Enoch's secret

So let us consider Enoch. What was his secret? It was three-fold.

Coming to God

The first answer is given in Hebrews 11:6, which is a commentary on verse 5: 'But without faith it is impossible to please him [God]: for he that cometh to God must believe that he is, and that he is a rewarder of them that diligently seek him.' We have seen that faith is always vital. But it is interesting to notice the way in which the writer puts it here. Using a most important phrase, he says, 'he that cometh to God'. This is an expression of which he is rather fond. He has already used it in the first verse of the tenth chapter where he is dealing with the whole question of how men and women are to approach God, how they may have access in worship into the presence of the everlasting and eternal God: 'For the law,' he says, 'having a shadow of good things to come, and not the very image of the things, can never with those sacrifices which they offered year by year continually make *the comers thereunto* perfect.'

Another phrase which indicates the same thought is found in Romans 5:1-2: 'Therefore being justified by faith, we have peace with God through our Lord Jesus Christ: by whom also we have *access by faith into this grace* wherein we stand, and rejoice in hope of the glory of God.' That is 'coming unto God'. It refers to men and women having access to God and being able to stand

33

before him in grace. It means access to God and his favour as we approach him in worship.

Those who come to God are anxious to have this access into his presence; this is the biggest thing in their lives. They do not attend church mechanically and then feel they have done their good deed for the day—wonderful, they go to church, whereas other people do not. No, no, those who 'come to God' do so that they may know him, that they may have access, that they may stand before him and have fellowship with him—that is the connotation of these words. So this is the first principle on which we must concentrate, and it was the great characteristic of Enoch: coming to God, entering into his presence. Is that true of us?

We are, therefore, faced with the question: How do we truly come to God? How do we really make sure that we have arrived, that we are in the Holiest of All, that we are speaking to God and that God is speaking to us? How does it happen? And the answer is given: 'He that cometh unto God must believe that he is, and that he is a rewarder of them that diligently seek him.'

Now there is no statement in the Scriptures, I think, that is more frequently misunderstood than this. It is generally interpreted like this: You cannot pray to God unless you believe in the existence and the being of God. Elementary! First principles! And furthermore, you must believe that if you live a good life and please him, God will reward you.

In other words, the popular interpretation of this verse is the popular notion of Christianity today. Christians are men and women who believe in God and who believe that if they live a good life, God will be pleased with them and they will go to heaven. So you believe in God and you believe that God is love. That is all, no more is necessary. Quite simple. 'Believe that he is, and that he is a rewarder of them that diligently seek him.'

But it is easy to show that not only is that wrong, but it is a blank contradiction of what the writer of Hebrews is teaching. It

34

is a contradiction of the whole of his epistle and of the whole teaching of the Bible. This verse has a much bigger and deeper and fuller meaning. Chapter 11 is about *faith*—the faith of these men and women of God, the faith that these Hebrew Christians should have in the light of the great doctrine that the writer has been expounding.

Faith

What is faith? Faith is *an acceptance of and a submission to the revelation of God.* 'Faith is the substance of things hoped for, the evidence of things not seen' (v.1). How do we know about these things? God has revealed them, and we accept the revelation.

So let us go on to the positive interpretation. Faith means, first, that we 'must believe that he [God] is'. This is the crucial phrase. When the writer says that we must believe that God is—and we can only do that, he says, by faith—he is contrasting faith with speculation. Many people speculate about God. They write books in which they claim that God is not 'up there' or 'out there'. Instead, God is 'depth'. But there is nothing like that in the Scriptures. This is modern man having come of age! He is now discovering God, as it were; he is giving a new description of him. But that sort of speculation is the antithesis of what we are told about Enoch.

That was the whole trouble, was it not, with those people to whom the apostle Paul was speaking in Athens? We are told that Paul addressed the Stoics and the Epicureans, and it is most interesting to notice what he says to them:

Paul stood in the midst of Mars' hill, and said, Ye men of Athens, I perceive that in all things ye are too superstitious [too religious]. For as I passed by, and beheld your devotions, I found an altar with this inscription, TO THE UNKNOWN

35

GOD. Whom therefore ye ignorantly worship, him declare I unto you (Acts 17:22-23).

That is the contrast. You see, these Athenians, these Stoics and Epicureans, were typical philosophers. They had a notion that there was some ultimate Being behind all their gods, behind all phenomena, and they were seeking 'if haply they might feel after him, and find him' (v.27). They were speculating, putting up theories and postulates, examining and arguing and debating and wrangling. 'Look here,' said Paul, 'you don't know what you're talking about': 'Whom you ignorantly worship'—this unknown God whom you don't know —'him *declare* I unto you.' That is the contrast.

In other words, faith means the acceptance of the revelation that God has given of himself. In effect, Paul was able to say to those Athenians, 'I am a Jew; and we Jews are not left with speculation based upon our own reason and understanding. God has revealed himself. He has chosen the nation of the Jews to receive the revelation, and we have it written down; we have the oracles of God. I am not theorising, but I am telling you what God has manifested concerning himself to the Jewish people, all he has done with that nation, and his purpose for the world.' Revelation! That is what it means.

But that is only the beginning. 'He that cometh to God must believe that he is.' Now surely there is a very profound and deep meaning here. This is surely a reference to that particular revelation which God gave of himself to Moses, and through him to the children of Israel. God had been giving revelations of himself to all the patriarchs—we have seen it already—to Adam, then to Abel and to Moses. We read:

And Moses said unto God, Behold, when I come unto the children of Israel, and shall say unto them, The God of your fathers hath

36

sent me unto you; and they shall say unto me, What is his name? what shall I say unto them? And God said unto Moses, I AM THAT I AM: and he said, Thus shalt thou say unto the children of Israel, I AM hath sent me unto you (Exodus 3:13-14).

Then notice the commentary on that passage which is given us in Exodus 6:

And God spake unto Moses, and said unto him, I am the LORD: and I appeared unto Abraham, unto Isaac, and unto Jacob, by the name of God Almighty, but by my name JEHOVAH [that is to say, 'I AM THAT I AM'] was I not known to them' (Exodus 6:2-3).

In these words, God gave a very special revelation to the children of Israel. Just before he was going to lead them out of the captivity of Egypt and take them to their promised land, he revealed himself as 'I am that I am' or 'I shall be what I shall be'. It is everything: I always was; I always shall be; I am. God is. And this is the special name, translated 'Jehovah' in the Authorised Version, that he always uses about himself when he wants to bring out his covenant relationship to his people. That is why he did it at that particular juncture. 'Thus shalt thou say . . . I AM hath sent me unto you': the God who has pledged himself to you, the God whose people you are, the God who is going to bring you to your promised land.

So we are told here that the first element in faith is the belief that God is, that he is the everlasting and eternal God, the God who has revealed himself to his people in covenant language and in covenant form, and who has a certain purpose with respect to them. Faith believes that; it submits to it. It says: 'I am not interested in the ideas of the latest philosopher, or the recent speculation of some clever fellow. No, no. All I know about God is what

I have in this book, the Bible. Here is God's revelation and I submit utterly, absolutely.' That is what Enoch did, and that is what all who have faith must, of necessity, do.

So the man of faith does not say, 'Ah, of course, we're modern people, we no longer believe in a Father God "up there". That's Victorian. Now, of course, we must think in scientific terms.' The moment people speak like that, I do not hesitate to say that they are not people of faith, but speculative philosophers. They may call themselves Christians—we cannot stop that—but they are not Christians. Christians are people of faith. They believe that God is what he has revealed himself to be. They know nothing apart from this revelation. That is the first element in faith.

Salvation

But then the writer adds to that. He says that God is 'a rewarder of them that diligently seek him'. This does not just mean that God is love and that God is kind. He is that, but the words mean much more. Here in this phrase we see again the whole content of the way of salvation. There are adumbrations of this in the Old Testament. 'But there is forgiveness with thee,' says the Psalmist, 'that thou mayest be feared' (Psalm 130:4). How did he know that? Did he just sit down and say, 'God must be a God of love because I cannot conceive of a God who is not prepared to forgive everybody and send everybody to heaven in the end'? No, no, that is speculation again. The Psalmist knows it because of the revelation.

'Whosoever shall call on the name of the Lord shall be saved' (Acts 2:21). How do I know that? Is it because I think it must be true because God is love? No, that is not the basis. It is because God has said so. 'He is a rewarder of them that diligently seek him.' This is the great theme of the Bible. This is what the saints of the Old Testament lived by. Now they did not see it as clearly as you and I should see it. 'Your father Abraham rejoiced to see

38

my day,' says our Lord, 'and he saw it, and was glad' (John 8:56). Indeed, at the end of Hebrews 11 we are similarly told that 'these all, having obtained a good report through faith, received not the promise' (v.39). And earlier in the chapter we are told specifically that these people did not see these things: 'These all died in faith, not having received the promises, but having seen them afar off, and were persuaded of them' (v.13).

In other words, all these Old Testament saints believed the revelation that God had given concerning his purpose of salvation. When we were looking at Abel, I reminded you that God had first announced this salvation in the Garden of Eden: '[The seed of the woman] shall bruise thy [the serpent's] head' (Genesis 3:5). It is all right, he said; there will be a conflict—'seed of the woman' and 'seed of the serpent'; life will be difficult, with thorns, briars, troubles and struggle, but I am giving you the promise that the seed of the woman will bruise the serpent's head. This would involve the Saviour being bruised in his heel, but that does not matter because there is the great promise, the purpose of God in salvation.

At the very dawn of history God made a proclamation, he gave a revelation. He addressed the man and woman in sin the moment they had fallen. He gave a kind of preview of history and said there would be a great division. God pronounced judgement upon sin. He said that he was a holy God who could not wink at sin. He denounced it and said that he would punish it. We have the specific statement of Jude to the effect that God had made this quite clear and that Enoch believed it:

Enoch also, the seventh from Adam, prophesied of these, saying, Behold, the Lord cometh with ten thousands of his saints, to execute judgment upon all, and to convince all that are ungodly among them of all their ungodly deeds which they have ungodly committed, and of all their hard speeches which ungodly sinners have spoken against him (verses 14-15).

Enoch believed that statement of God. He believed that God would judge the world in righteousness and punish sinners by banishing them out of his sight eternally.

But then God gives the offer of salvation, he announces his purpose of redemption; and these two, salvation and destruction, run right through the whole of the Bible. And Enoch believed the message of salvation, and gave himself to it. He believed that God *is*—this covenant God, this God of the promise, this God of the purpose, this God of the way of salvation. He believed the two sides—judgement and redemption—and he submitted himself to it.

That is what faith means. Men and women of faith believe that God is, and that he is a rewarder of them that diligently seek him. They submit themselves absolutely to the revelation of God and his gracious purpose. Enoch trusted God's word utterly and based the whole of his life upon it. That is the first thing.

Diligently seeking

Without faith you cannot begin. Nothing can be done at all. That is why 'the world by wisdom knew not God' (1 Corinthians 1:21). Enoch's secret lay, firstly, in his faith, and then, secondly, in the fact that he sought God diligently. We are told that '[God] is a rewarder of them that *diligently* seek him.' Now the Authorised (KJV) translation here is right; it is good. The New English Bible, so-called, puts it: 'he rewards those who search for him'. But these words mean much more than just searching for God. There is something special about this seeking. There is the notion of constantly taking trouble to find him out.

The Christian does not just say, 'Oh yes, of course I believe in God, I've always believed in him. I was brought up to believe in God. I never go to a place of worship, but I say my prayers.' That is not Christianity. That is not the attitude of the child of God. Christians not only know how to seek him, but they go on seeking him.

40

In a sense, the whole secret of Enoch was not just that while so many were godless and vile and evil round and about him in the ancient world, he believed in God and lived a good life, but that he diligently sought God. Enoch did not just announce, 'Of course, I wouldn't dream of doing those evil things!' while living a nice little quiet respectable life, saying, 'I believe in God and this is my kind of life.' No, he sought God because he enjoyed him, because he wanted fellowship with him. He did not just spend five minutes in the morning reading a little portion of Scripture and a comment on it and then a little prayer, and after that dismiss God. He did not say, 'I've done my daily portion, I'm right with God', and then go on with his life without another thought of God. No, no, he sought God, he wanted to realise his presence, he was looking for him always, everywhere, at all times.

And that is what we are to do. 'But as many as received him, to them gave he power to become the sons of God [the children of God]' (John 1:12), and the child has access to the Father's presence. When servants are not allowed, the master is always ready to receive his child. And the child wants to be there; he wants to be near his Father, and he is not happy when he is away. This was the big factor in the life of Enoch; he was not happy when he was not enjoying the active, full, conscious presence of God, so he sought him diligently. He was always seeking; he was always turning to him in thought, in meditation, and in prayer. It was the whole tenor of his life.

Walking with God

And then the third thing we are told about Enoch is that 'he walked with God' (Genesis 5:22). The full life of faith is described in these verses about Enoch. We have looked at the devotional and experiential aspects, and now we come to the practical outworking of faith: 'Enoch walked with God.' This tells us a great deal about the type of life Enoch was living. Enoch always

41

realised that he was living in the presence of God—which is what walking with God means. He had a conscious sense of the presence of God.

Let me divide this up as John divided it up for us in the first chapter of his first epistle. Like the writer of the Epistle to the Hebrews, John was also writing to give believers assurance. He says, 'These things write we unto you, that your joy may be full' (1 John 1:4). So how are we to get this full joy? Here it is: 'This then is the message which we have heard of him, and declare unto you, that God is light, and in him is no darkness at all' (1 John 1:5).

Men and women who walk with God always say to themselves, 'Wherever I go, God is. I can never go out of his presence.' Work that out in terms of Psalm 139: 'If I ascend up into heaven, thou art there: if I make my bed in hell, behold, thou art there. If I take the wings of the morning, and dwell in the uttermost parts of the sea; even there shall thy hand lead me' (Psalm 139:8-10). God is everywhere. Those who walk with God remind themselves of that and are conscious of it. Of course, they can do things in secret, unseen by other people. Their wives or husbands and their Cabinet colleagues[1] may not see them. But God sees them. Christians know that they are always, everywhere, in his presence.

Christians also walk in the consciousness that 'God is light, and in him is no darkness at all.' Their chief desire is to please God. They know that our Lord has told us: 'He that hath my commandments, and keepeth them, he it is that loveth me' (John 14:21). Love is not an empty sentiment. If you love a person you want to please that person. If you love God you want to please God, and you please him by keeping his commandments.

Or, to put it negatively, those who walk with God avoid everything that displeases him. Listen to John again: 'God is light, and in him is no darkness at all. If we say that we have fellowship with

---

1 This was the time of the 'Profumo scandal' in London.

him, and walk in darkness, we lie, and do not the truth' (1 John
1:5-6). So if you are walking with God you are not walking in
the darkness, you are walking in the light. If you say that you are
in fellowship with him, and in the meantime are walking in
darkness, you are a liar! You are not deceiving God, but you are
deceiving yourself, and if you are a true man or woman of God
you do not want to do that.

John puts it another way in chapter 2: 'Love not the world,
neither the things that are in the world' (v.15). We know what they
are, do we not? They are constantly plastered before us in the
newspapers and on our television screens.

Love not the world, neither the things that are in the world.
If any man love the world, the love of the Father is not in
him. For all that is in the world, the lust of the flesh, and the
lust of the eyes, and the pride of life, is not of the Father, but
is of the world. And the world passeth away, and the lust
thereof: but he that doeth the will of God abideth for ever
(1 John 2:15-17).

So those who walk with God avoid these wrong things. They
hate the world because they love God and they want to be well
pleasing in his sight. And should they inadvertently fall into sin,
they are heartbroken.

Do you treat yourselves lightly when you fall into sin, or does
it grieve you that you have sinned against this God who loved you
so much that he sent his only Son to die for you? Does your sin
grieve you, does it get you down? It should. But you do not
remain on the ground, you repeat the words of 1 John 1:7: 'If we
walk in the light, as he is in the light, we have fellowship one with
another, and the blood of Jesus Christ his Son cleanseth us from
all sin.' The men and women who walk with God believe those
words. Further, they believe that 'If we confess our sins, he is

43

faithful and just to forgive us our sins, and to cleanse us from all unrighteousness' (v.9). So they do not say, 'I've ceased to be a Christian, I might as well give up.' They say, 'No, I'll go back to him, I'll go to my Father.' They confess their sin and accept and believe that they are completely forgiven and cleansed anew and afresh, and they get up and go on walking with God in the light.

'Come with me!'

Enoch's secret has been the secret of every child of God in every age and generation. Is it ours? Do you know what it is to walk consciously with God? Is this the height of our ambition, whatever the world may do or say? Is it our greatest concern to enjoy his companionship, to be well pleasing in his sight? It was because Enoch was like that, that God translated him.

I rather like the way an old Welsh preacher used to put this. He would say:

Here was this man, Enoch, walking with God. Every day he would go and look for God, and they would have a walk together. And then God would say, 'Well, I must leave you now; you go home and sleep. Get up in the morning and do your work and I will look out for you again tomorrow.'

This was the life that Enoch lived [said the preacher]. This was his greatest delight. Enoch had his work to do, of course, but he always looked for the times when he could give himself utterly and absolutely to taking a walk with God and enjoying his companionship.

He had been enjoying this every day, as we are told in the record, for several hundred years. Then one day he finished his work and went as usual to the meeting-place where God was waiting for him, and they walked together, and it was wonderful. God had never been so loving, he had never been so kind, and Enoch had never been so happy.

44

The time came, the usual time, for God to say, 'Very well, I must leave it at that for today, and we will meet again tomorrow.' But on this occasion God did not say that. He said, 'Enoch, we have been doing this together now for so long. You enjoy it; I enjoy it. Tonight, I am not going to say to you, "Go home and rest and sleep and get up and do your work and look for me tomorrow." Enoch,' he said, 'do not go home. Come with me!'

So God took him and he was not. God took him to his everlasting habitation. The perpetual fellowship was to be absolute. There was never to be another break or another intermission.

All right, that was an old preacher's imagination, but there is a profound truth in it. You and I should have such an intimate knowledge of God that it really more or less comes to that. And what is death? Well, death just becomes this: that God says to us, 'All right, I am not going to leave you in this old world any longer. Come along, come to me permanently! Come into the everlasting habitation that my beloved Son has prepared for you. Come home, come with me, and be with me for the remainder of eternity, for everlasting life, for endless living in my presence. Come home!'

3
Abraham:
friendship with God

*'But as many as received him, to them gave he power to
become the sons of God, even to them that believe on his name:
which were born, not of blood, nor of the will of the flesh,
nor of the will of man, but of God.'*
(John 1:12-13)

*'By faith Abraham, when he was called to go out
into a place which he should after receive for an
inheritance, obeyed; and he went out, not knowing whither he
went. By faith he sojourned in the land of promise,as in a
strange country, dwelling in tabernacles with Isaac and Jacob,
the heirs with him of the same promise: for he looked
for a city which hath foundations, whose builder and maker is
God. Through faith also Sarah herself received strength to
conceive seed, and was delivered of a child when she was
past age, because she judged him faithful who
had promised. Therefore sprang there even of one,
and him as good as dead, so many as the stars of the
sky in multitude, and as the sand which is by the
sea shore innumerable.'*
(Hebrews 11:8-12)

Now we come to the great story of Abraham. Once more, the
thing that strikes us is that while the fundamental principle

47

controlling the life of all these people was precisely the same— this faith, this assurance—in each case there is some special feature. That is where the writer of the letter to the Hebrews shows himself to be such a profound teacher. He does not merely say, 'Look back across the Old Testament and you will find that your fathers all lived by the principle of faith.' No, he picks out certain salient truths about each one. His reason for doing this is that these people all differed in many respects. They differed temperamentally and in their immediate circumstances. And he knows that we, too, are different in many ways. So he gives us some details about them all in order that somewhere or another he may include our case, our special position, and thereby give the comfort that we need.

Assurance of faith

Now here, once more, the big principle is that Abraham lived as he did and was the man he was because he had an absolute certainty about his relationship to God and about God's purpose for him. That was his secret. He did some extraordinary, wonderful things. Yes, but he was enabled to do them because he *knew*, he had an assurance of salvation, a great assurance of faith and hope.

This is something that we are told repeatedly concerning Abraham. Before he ever left his old home, the place where he had been brought up and where his forefathers had always lived, he was given an assurance in these words: 'The LORD had said unto Abram, Get thee out of thy country, and from thy kindred, and from thy father's house, unto a land that I will shew thee: and I will make of thee a great nation, and I will bless thee, and make thy name great' (Genesis 12:1-2).

God gave Abraham this assurance. That is the principle that runs right through the story of Abraham. This promise is repeated in Genesis 15:1: 'After these things the word of the LORD came unto Abram in a vision, saying, Fear not, Abram: I am thy shield, and thy exceeding great reward.' And it occurs several other times, in chapters 17 and 18, and so on.

This is a most important principle. This is what I am trying to inculcate. It is the whole teaching. The highest form of assurance is not an assurance that you deduce yourself from the Scriptures, it is an assurance that is given to you by God. 'The Spirit itself beareth witness with our spirit, that we are the children of God' (Romans 8:16). This is the assurance that every Christian should be enjoying, the assurance that gives power and fullness of joy. It was this that turned John Wesley from a halting believer into a new man. Before that point, he had certainly been a Christian, but one who was uncertain, a miserable failure in the ministry. The moment he was given the assurance that his sins, even his, had been forgiven, he was transformed; he was filled with power. It was the same with Luther, and with Whitefield. It is the same with all the great Christian leaders.

The friend of God

But there is something even further. We find it in the Epistle of James: 'And the Scripture was fulfilled which saith, Abraham believed God, and it was imputed unto him for righteousness: and he was called the Friend of God' (James 2:23). Now that is wonderful. We have seen that Enoch 'walked with God', and we looked at something of the content of that. But here we are told that Abraham was called the friend of God.

James is referring to a statement made several times in different places in the Old Testament where Abraham is referred to as the friend of God. And there is no doubt but that God had made this clear to Abraham himself. A friend is one to whom you tell your intimate secrets. You can have acquaintances with whom you are civil. When you meet, you are happy together and they enjoy your company. But they are not friends. The friend is the one whom you take, as it were, into your bosom, to whom you open

49

your heart, the one you can trust. Friendship! It is the highest relationship that is possible between men and women outside marriage. Thus we find that Abraham was the friend of God, and we have ample proof of the fact that he was treated as a friend.

If you read those great chapters in Genesis about Abraham, you will find that generally God called Abraham to him and said, as it were, 'I want to tell you something.' Take that time when God told Abraham what he was going to do to Sodom and Gomorrah. He did not destroy those cities without telling Abraham. Abraham was given a warning beforehand; he was told all about it; he was let into the secret. And God was always dealing with Abraham in that way.

In Old Testament times

Now this case of Abraham does make us pause for a moment to look at some of the ways in which this assurance was given in Old Testament times: it is a subject of great interest. How did God let these people know? There were various ways.

By visions. We are told in Genesis 15:1: 'The word of the LORD came unto Abram in a vision.' The Holy Spirit was not given then as he is given now, so God at times gave assurance by giving a vision. Now to see a vision is not to see the actual thing, but the appearance, the representation of something. And many of the Old Testament saints were given these visions—none perhaps more than Abraham.

By dreams. You must have noticed that you do not find this so much in the New Testament, but in the Old Testament there are endless illustrations of God speaking through dreams. Someone would wake up and say, 'What has been happening?' God had spoken. He had given some intimation of something that he was going to do, or wanted that person to do.

In a theophany. Another very striking way in which God revealed his purposes was by theophanies. These were appearances of God, and especially of the Lord Jesus Christ. When the

50

three men came to Abraham to tell him about the destruction of
Sodom and Gomorrah, the one who spoke was the Lord Jesus
Christ, not incarnate, but in an appearance. Before he was born
as the babe of Bethlehem, he had come in the guise of an angel,
in the form of a man sometimes, and had spoken to people like
Abraham.

By impressions upon the mind. And then, in addition, impressions were made upon the mind by the Holy Spirit. Undoubtedly
something like that happened to the prophets when they said, 'The
word of the Lord came.'

In the New Testament era

So here is the whole argument, it seems to me, of this author of
the Epistle to the Hebrews. He says: If God gave assurance to
those Old Testament saints, how much more will he give assurance to you! God dealt with the Old Testament saints in those
ways because that was, as it were, the only way in which he could
speak to them and give them assurance, but now you are in a very
different position. The incarnation has taken place, the Son of
God has been here among us, he has taken not the nature of
angels but the seed of Abraham. He has been a man among men
and has died upon the cross. He has finished the work, and the
Spirit has been given in a way that he had never been given
before.

The prophecy in John 7:37-39 has actually taken place. There
we are told: 'The Holy Ghost was not yet given; because that
Jesus was not yet glorified.' But Jesus *is* now glorified and the
Spirit has been given. He has been poured out upon all flesh, and
there has never been such a profusion. But the deduction you
should draw from all that, says this writer of the letter to the
Hebrews, is that if the Old Testament saints, who simply saw these
things afar off, had the assurance that they had, and if they
rejoiced in it, and if they were able to walk in the strength of it and

51

triumph and prevail in spite of the world, the flesh and the devil, how much more should you be able to rejoice, you who are in this new dispensation, in this Christian era, in these times when the ends of the world are come upon us!

And the same argument applies to us. We also are in a position that is superior to that of Abraham and all these others who are mentioned here, because we are living in the New Testament era. Therefore the question we must ask ourselves is this: Are we enjoying this great assurance? Are we able to walk as Abraham walked in this evil world? He did it because he had the assurance; do we have it? Has the Holy Spirit testified with our spirits that we are the children of God? Are we rejoicing in the Lord? Are we so sure of these things that nothing can daunt us and frustrate us?

Learning from Abraham

It is fascinating for any preacher—and all of you who are students of the Word have, I am sure, felt the same fascination—to notice the things the author has pinpointed out of the story of Abraham. It is very interesting to see his selection. He does not give a complete account of Abraham; no, he has a point to make, he is illustrating one thing, and out of the rich history that is found there in Genesis he picks out the elements that help to illustrate his point. And we must follow him because we, too, are concerned about the selfsame point.

What details, then, does the writer emphasise? I have tried to classify them under two main headings.

Abraham's characteristics

What was it that made Abraham the man he was? Why was he called the friend of God? Why did these great things happen to him? Why is he called the father of all the faithful? Christians are described in the Epistle to the Galatians as 'the seed of Abraham'; all the children of faith are the children of Abraham; he is the great exemplar of the life of faith. So what were his characteristics?

He believed God

The first is, of course, that statement that is always made about him: 'Abraham believed God' (Galatians 3:6). That was the secret; that was the fundamental point. Faith, in the end, simply means that a man and woman believe God. They believe everything that God has said, everything that God has prophesied, everything that God has been pleased to reveal. They believe and they submit to it. And Abraham did that.

But in particular, of course, Abraham believed God *concerning his great purpose.* This is a wonderful theme that runs right through the Bible. We have already seen, away back in the case of Abel in contrast with Cain, that this became the fundamental dividing point in the whole human race. God made that perfect world and set Adam and Eve in it, and all was paradise, it was perfect, and God looked upon it and saw that it was good. But in their folly Adam and Eve rebelled and sinned and brought chaos down.

And God came down, you remember, and in that statement in the Garden of Eden he gave a preview of history and the first intimation of his purpose. He said that there would be terrible warfare between the seed of the woman and the seed of the serpent. That was the punishment of this sin. But—and here is the purpose of God—the seed of the woman would bruise the serpent's head (Genesis 3:15). And the Bible is nothing but an account of God's plan of redemption, the preparation of it, the carrying out of it, and the application of it.

Now the essence, of course, of Christianity and of salvation is belief in this fundamental proposition. The whole test of every man and woman who comes into this world is whether they believe that and allow it to control every aspect of their lives. And the great thing about Abraham is that he did. He was a man who

53

had been brought up in paganism—Ur of the Chaldees was a pagan society—but God spoke to him, and Abraham believed God. And it was as the result of that that everything else followed.

God's plan of salvation is sometimes put in terms of a covenant. When God came to Abraham and told him that through him all the nations of the earth would be blessed, Abraham realised that that was not merely a statement about physical events, but also had a very great spiritual content. He realised that God was speaking in the whole context of salvation.

The repetition of the word 'covenant' in both the Old Testament and the New helps us to grasp the great point that God reveals himself, his own character, and his purpose with respect to this world and its people; and he reveals that it is a purpose of salvation. That is why the apostle Paul writes to the Christians in Rome: 'We know that all things work together for good to them that love God, to them who are the called according to his purpose' (Romans 8:28). God's purpose determines everything, and all who are called according to this purpose are the children of God. Abraham was told this and he believed it.

In other words, Abraham *believed God when he told him that in paganism he was lost and under condemnation,* and *he believed God when he told him that no man could save himself.* However good people may be, and however excellent their works, it is all insufficient in the sight of God. So Paul wrote: 'Abraham believed God, and it was accounted to him for righteousness' (Galatians 3:6). That is why Abraham is the father, as it were, of all who believe in justification by faith only, and that is why his example is so frequently used as an argument in the New Testament. The apostle Paul devotes almost the whole of chapter 4 of the Epistle to the Romans to this one case of Abraham, and it is used by both James and the author of Hebrews.

There is nothing more vital than the doctrine of justification by faith only. Very many people in the Church are unhappy because they think they have to justify themselves—anyone who thinks like that is sooner or later bound to be miserable. If people look honestly at themselves, they do not feel satisfied; if they look at the saints, they feel that they themselves are nobodies who have never done a thing; if they look into the face of Christ they are overwhelmed; if they have a glimpse of the judgement of the holy law of God, they realise that their whole condition is in jeopardy. What can they do? And the answer is the revelation of God— God's purpose of justification by faith in Christ.

Let me show you how our Lord himself taught this in a most interesting manner. This is the very essence of the meaning of the words, 'Abraham believed God.' Our Lord said, 'Your father Abraham rejoiced to see my day: and he saw it, and was glad' (John 8:56). In other words, God had revealed to Abraham how he was going to carry out his purpose of redemption. Let us never forget that; it is a most crucial statement. These Old Testament saints had been given a preview of all that was to happen in Christ. We are told here in Hebrews 11 that they only saw it 'afar off' (v.13). They did not fully understand, but they saw enough to rejoice.

God said to Abraham: 'When the fullness of the time has come I will send my own Son. I will make him a man and put the sins of all humanity upon him. I will smite him and punish sin in him. He is the way of redemption and all who believe in him will be saved, and all who do not believe in him will be lost.' That was the message: the grand purpose of God in Christ was to save those who believe. Justification by faith only! 'Not of works, lest any man should boast' (Ephesians 2:9).

Abraham believed God. He *believed God's purpose of salvation and of redemption.* He became a man of faith. It is very important for us to realise that. Faith is not walking in the dark, whistling to keep up its courage. Faith is believing God! It is not a vague hope. Faith knows what it believes. 'Faith is the substance of things hoped for, the evidence of things not seen.'

55

Abraham also *believed all God said about life in this world, and life in the world to come.* 'He looked for a city which hath foundations, whose builder and maker is God' (v.10). Abraham believed God when he said: 'In this world people are divided into two groups. Which group do you belong to? I call you to listen and consider. You must come out of paganism; you must live the life that I have planned for you. You are to be one of my people.'

This word challenges us about our attitude to life in this world. The men we have looked at have all been separated from the world. They were in it but they did not belong to it. Abraham was taken right out, and he went very gladly.

He obeyed God

Abraham's second characteristic, and this is very important, is that he obeyed God. And that is the point that is made by James when he refers to Abraham in chapter 2 of his epistle. There is no contradiction between Paul and James: they emphasise the two sides of the one great truth. Paul's message is that works are of no value, that we are justified by faith only. And James then puts his emphasis rightly on the fact that 'faith if it hath not works is dead' (James 2:17). James shows the way to differentiate between a mechanical believism, or an intellectual acceptance of the truth, and a real belief. When you have true faith, you put into practice what you say you believe.

And so we have to emphasise the fact that Abraham obeyed God. There is something tremendous about this; this is where the Scriptures are so wonderful. And yet you and I, in rushing through our daily portion of Scripture, so often miss these essential and central glories. Take the statement in Genesis 12, this laconic remark that is nevertheless so pregnant with profound meaning:

The LORD had said unto Abram, Get thee out of thy country, and from thy kindred, and from thy father's house, unto a land that I will shew thee: and I will make of thee a great nation, and I will bless thee, and make thy name great; and thou shalt be a blessing: and I will bless them that bless thee, and curse him that curseth thee: and in thee shall all families of the earth be blessed. So *Abram departed, as the Lord had spoken unto him* (Genesis 12:1-4).

And that is all we are told. God said, 'Come out!' And Abraham went out!

That is what the author of Hebrews emphasises: 'By faith Abraham, when he was called to go out into a place which he should after receive for an inheritance, obeyed; and he went out, not knowing whither he went' (v.8). It is not a small thing suddenly to get up and leave the place in which your forefathers lived. You leave all your associations, your relatives and your friends. And every true Christian knows something about that. There is a separation. You leave your background; you leave what you were by nature; you step out. That is faith! That is obeying the call of God unto salvation and redemption. It is a departing, a cutting loose, a forsaking of something, and a walking out into that to which God is calling you, whatever the consequences, whatever the cost. '[Abraham] obeyed; and he went out, not knowing whither he went.'

He sought to please God

That leads me to the third great characteristic of this man, the last which seems to me to be emphasised here. Abraham's greatest aim was to please God and to be blessed by God. Read again Abraham's story as it is given in Genesis and you will find that this was always the big thing in Abraham's mind.

We read in Genesis of a dispute between Abraham and Lot, his companion and relative. As they were journeying on, they saw some land before them. There was the fertile plain on which were the cities of Sodom and Gomorrah, and there were the hills. Abraham was senior to Lot and had the right of first choice. But he did not take it. He could see the fruitful plain, but he could also see Sodom and Gomorrah. Lot could not see the condition of Sodom and Gomorrah and he chose them. He wanted wealth and all that belonged to an affluent life. He chose the richer land, while Abraham was content to keep his sheep on the hilltops.

Abraham was able to take that decision because he always had his eye on God. 'He looked for a city which hath foundations, whose builder and maker is God.' He did not live for this life, for this world. He had his flocks and he was a wealthy man, but he could have been much richer. His secret was: God first. He was always out to please God.

Later on, we find another illustration. Abraham rescued Lot from the kings who had attacked Sodom and Gomorrah, and he was also able to deliver certain southern kings from the same enemy. The king of Sodom therefore wanted to give him a very great reward, but Abraham refused it. What he had done he had done for God. God said to him, 'I am thy shield, and thy exceeding great reward' (Genesis 15:1). And he had conquered his enemies because God had been his shield; but God was also his 'exceeding great reward'. He did not want any reward from a king like the king of Sodom. No, no! God was sufficient. God was first. Abraham was always animated by that great moving and controlling idea.

Those, then, very briefly, are the characteristics of Abraham; they made him the man he was.

The blessings of assurance

And now we come to consider the second point. The greatest blessing of all that assurance brings us is the knowledge of God; we know his character. There is all the difference in the world between believing things about God and really knowing him. Now assurance gives that knowledge. God speaks to people, he reveals his secrets, and in so doing he gives a revelation of himself.

Knowing God

We can see this clearly in that one great phrase used by Abraham in addressing God over the question of Sodom and Gomorrah: 'Shall not the Judge of all the earth do right?' (Genesis 18:25). You see, Abraham knew God! Abraham, as it were, said to God, 'Whatever you are going to do, I know you will never do any wrong. I have come to know you. You are a righteous God, a holy God, and you are a just God.' He had been taken into the intimacy and he had an understanding of the character and the nature and the being of God.

The apostle Paul has a wonderful way of putting this in Romans 4, where he deals with the birth of Isaac, the child promised to Abraham and Sarah when they were both over ninety. We are told that Abraham 'staggered not at the promise of God through unbelief'. Why was this? It was because he 'was . . . giving the glory to God' (Romans 4:20). He did not stagger in unbelief at the promise given him because he knew God. He knew the greatness of God and the power of God and the immutability of God's counsel. He knew that when God promises, he also performs. He never fails, and his promises are ever sure.

Oh, in this wilderness which we call life in this world, there is nothing more important than to know God, to know his character, to know that God is who he is, the everlasting, unchanging God, 'the Father of lights, with whom is no variableness, neither shadow of turning' (James 1:17); 'the God of all grace' (1 Peter 5:10); 'the God and Father of our Lord Jesus Christ' (2 Corinthians 11:31).

Beloved people, do you know God? Do you know God's character? Are you certain about him? I say again, the first great blessing of assurance is that it brings us to a knowledge of God. You do not believe at a distance; you do not even have to rely upon the revelation given in the Bible. You start with the revelation, but over and above that, God underlines it, authenticates it, makes it absolute, so that there is no question at all.

Trusting God

But then assurance leads to a complete trust in God, and you will have this trust, come what may. Now we are told that about Abraham in two main respects. First, Abraham trusted God even though he did not understand what God was doing with him. This is most important. 'By faith Abraham, when he was called to go out into a place which he should after receive for an inheritance, obeyed; and he went out, not knowing whither he went.' He had no idea where he was going, but he went.

Why did Abraham go? Fortunately, I need not expatiate on this; an old Puritan of three hundred years ago said it all perfectly in one of those pithy phrases that was so characteristic of the Puritans: 'Abraham went out,' he said, 'not knowing whither he went, but he knew with whom he was going!' And if you know with whom you are going, you need not bother about the destination. It does not matter where he leads you, whether the way be light or dark, you can always trust him.

Abraham did not want to know where he was going. All he needed to know was that he was going with God. The way was uncertain, it was dark, it was unknown, but what did that matter? He was going with God, and as long as he was with God, nothing disturbed him, nothing gave him anxiety.

Secondly, Abraham trusted God even when the promises of God were not immediately fulfilled. That is brought out in a most interesting way in verses 9 and 10: 'By faith he sojourned in the land of promise, as in a strange country, dwelling in tabernacles with Isaac and Jacob, the heirs with him of the same promise: for he looked for a city which hath foundations, whose builder and maker is God.' I wonder whether we see the full significance of that? Why does the writer say that Abraham 'sojourned' in the land of promise? A sojourner does not settle down in one place, but lives there for the time being, on a temporary lease, as it were. That is the difference between a sojourner and a tenant. The only dwelling that Abraham ever had in Canaan was a tent. He dwelt in tents, as did those others who were heirs with him of the promise, Isaac and Jacob.

What is the significance of that? Well, to find the answer you must go to Stephen's speech in Acts.

> Then said the high priest, Are these things so? And he [Stephen] said, Men, brethren, and fathers, hearken; The God of glory appeared unto our father Abraham, when he was in Mesopotamia, before he dwelt in Charran, and said unto him, Get thee out of thy country, and from thy kindred, and come into the land which I shall shew thee. Then came he out of the land of the Chaldaeans, and dwelt in Charran: and from thence, when his father was dead, he removed him into this land [Palestine, the land of Canaan], wherein ye now dwell. *And he gave him none inheritance in it, no, not so much as to set his foot on: yet he promised that he would give it to him for a possession, and to his seed after him, when as yet he had no child* (Acts 7:1-5).

Now that is astounding. You remember that we read in Genesis that God had said to Abraham: 'And I will give unto thee, and to thy seed after thee, the land wherein thou art a stranger, all the land of Canaan, for an everlasting possession' (Genesis 17:8). But we read in Acts 7:5: 'And he gave him none inheritance in it . . . yet he promised.' Furthermore, the author of Hebrews says: 'By faith he sojourned in the land of promise, as in a strange country' (v.9). The astonishing thing about Abraham is that he believed God! Though the promise was not actually fulfilled in his own

61

day, he knew it was true. He knew the land was his. He knew it would belong to his descendants, even though he himself was not given it as an actual possession and he merely sojourned there.

Now a man lacking in faith might so easily have said, 'Ah, but when you spoke to me you said that you were going to give it me, and you haven't.' But Abraham never said that. He did not fully understand God's purpose, but he said: This is all right. This is his way. I will walk it whatever it is. Nothing matters to me except his word. I know he is going to fulfil it in his own time and in his own way. It is sufficient for me that he has brought me here, and I know that my posterity will possess the land.

So, one of the greatest blessings of assurance is that even when God's promises do not seem to be fulfilled and one's way is dark, it is quite all right. You are able to say with Abraham:

> *God moves in a mysterious way*
> *His wonders to perform;*
> *He plants His footsteps in the sea,*
> *And rides upon the storm.*

You do not understand this, but:

> *Ye fearful saints, fresh courage take:*
> *The clouds ye so much dread*
> *Are big with mercy, and shall break*
> *In blessings on your head.*

> *Judge not the Lord by feeble sense,*
> *But trust Him for His grace;*
> *Behind a frowning Providence*
> *He hides a Father's face.*
>
> William Cowper

This is what comes out so gloriously and so wonderfully in this case of Abraham.

My dear friend, are you enjoying the blessings of assurance? Do you know him? Do you trust him in the dark? Do you 'hope against hope', as Abraham did? Do you believe his promises, always, or do you sometimes go to him grumbling and complaining? Do you say, 'Where are your promises? Why haven't you fulfilled them?' Do you ever go to God with a grudge and feel he is not true and is harsh with you? God have mercy upon us if we do!

Christians are meant to be men and women who know that they are children of God. They are meant to know their Father, and they are meant to know him so thoroughly that whatever happens they are able to say, 'All my God ordains is right—all things, whatever they are.'

'All things [without exception] work together for good to them that love God, to them who are the called according to his purpose' (Romans 8:28). God grant that we may all have and enjoy this blessed assurance, that we might be the friends of God to whom he speaks and reveals himself, and gives his intimacies, and grants the full assurance that we are his, and that he is ours!

4
Abraham:
faith tested

'But as many as received him, to them gave he power
to become the sons of God, even to them that believe on his
name: which were born, not of blood, nor of the will of
the flesh, nor of the will of man, but of God.'
(John 1:12-13)

'By faith Abraham, when he was tried, offered up Isaac:
and he that had received the promises offered up his
only begotten son, of whom it was said, That in Isaac
shall thy seed be called: accounting that God was able
to raise him up, even from the dead; from whence
also he received him in a figure.'
(Hebrews 11:17-19)

At the beginning of Hebrews chapter 12, the author writes: 'Wherefore seeing we also are compassed about with so great a cloud of witnesses, let us lay aside every weight, and the sin which doth so easily beset us, and let us run with patience the race that is set before us.' As we have been seeing, you cannot run the race that is set before you with patience, unless you have assurance. Chapter 11 of Hebrews is the great chapter on assurance. Here we see it in practice, here are the illustrations. So we have been looking at these great and glorious examples, and we are now considering Abraham.

Abraham is a very remarkable and striking case, and more space is given to him than to anybody else. That is not surprising; he is, after all, 'the father of all them that believe' (Romans 4:11): as Christians we are all the children of Abraham because we are the children of faith. And in the Bible the first illustration of anything is always given with great thoroughness. The first example is always put particularly plainly, and then you see how the others conform to it.

When we looked at verses 8 to 12, we saw that the great characteristics of this man were that he believed God, that he obeyed him and that his supreme desire was to please him, and we saw some of the blessings that followed from that. We saw that the secret of Abraham's life was his assurance of his relationship to God. 'Faith', after all, 'is the substance of things hoped for, the evidence of things not seen' (Hebrews 11:1). Now that is assurance.

All the men and women in Hebrews 11 had a wonderful assurance of their relationship to God, and it was this that enabled them to do all that they did. So the argument is this: If that was possible for them, it should be equally possible for us. Indeed, it ought to be more possible for us. 'These all', as the writer says here in the thirteenth verse, 'died in faith, not having received the promises, but having seen them afar off.' But you and I can look back to the fulfilment of the promises. You and I are living in an age when the Spirit has been poured forth in great abundance. We live in the post-Pentecost era. So if they in their day and generation could enjoy this assurance, how much more should we! And it is as potent an argument today as it was when this Epistle to the Hebrews was written.

Are we enjoying assurance of salvation? Are we able to rise to the height of these great men and women? The purpose of Hebrews 11 is to bring us to that. Therefore we are trying to discover what it was that enabled these people to live as they did.

What is it that characterises people who enjoy this great assurance, and what happens to them as the result?

When we looked at verses 8 to 12 of Hebrews 11, we saw that Abraham's faith was so great that when, at the age of ninety-nine, he was told by God that he and Sarah, who was over ninety herself, were to have a child, a son, and that it was through this child that the line was to be continued and blessings were to come to all the nations of the world—when he was given this promise, 'Abraham staggered not . . . through unbelief; but was strong in faith, giving glory to God' (Romans 4:20). And this is astounding.

But now the author continues. He has a short digression in verses 13 to 16 in which, as a very wise teacher, he interrupts himself, as it were, and says: 'Now I hope you are following the argument; I hope you are seeing the point I am making.' He says it is this:

> These all died in faith, not having received the promises, but having seen them afar off, and were persuaded of them, and embraced them, and confessed that they were strangers and pilgrims on the earth. For they that say such things declare plainly that they seek a country. And truly, if they had been mindful of that country from whence they came out, they might have had opportunity to have returned. But now they desire a better country, that is, an heavenly: wherefore God is not ashamed to be called their God: for he hath prepared for them a city (Hebrews 11:13-16).

These words are a summary. We know that the author is not going right back to the beginning because he says that all these people died in faith, and Enoch did not die, as we saw. He is referring to Abraham and Sarah, Isaac and Jacob; and that, he says, is the truth about them.

The writer goes on: 'By faith'—back he comes to Abraham—'by faith Abraham, when he was tried, offered up Isaac: and he that had received the promises offered up his only begotten son, of whom it was said, That in Isaac shall thy seed be called.'

'Now,' says the writer in effect, 'I have more to say about Abraham.' That is why I emphasised at the beginning that Abraham is, perhaps, the most striking case of all the saints of the Old Testament. He is certainly the most striking in this eleventh chapter of Hebrews. Here is faith in action; here is 'the father of the faithful'; here is the pioneer, if you like, of justification by faith only—though, as we have seen, the principle was already in operation earlier, in the case of Abel. But here it is defined and set forth in a particularly clear and obvious manner.

The nature of assurance

And so the writer gives us a further detail concerning Abraham, and it is to this that I want to call your attention now. We are shown something about the nature of assurance here, in this most extraordinary incident, which stands out in the whole of the Bible, with all its histories and stories, as one of the most remarkable events of all.

God suddenly came to Abraham one day when, according to the first-century Jewish historian Josephus, Isaac was about twenty-five years old, and told him to take his son Isaac and offer him up as a burnt offering. Abraham had to take wood with him and have material ready to light a fire. He had to build an altar, lay the wood on it, bind Isaac and kill him on the altar, and then offer him up as a burnt offering to God.

And we are told that by faith Abraham did as he was commanded. It is summed up here in the words, 'Abraham, when he was tried, offered up Isaac' (v.17). As we know, Abraham did not actually kill Isaac, but he would have killed him if he had not been stopped.

68

Now, on any showing, Abraham's obedience to God's command is one of the most amazing events that has ever happened to a human being; and, remember, the whole purpose of chronicling it is that we might know something about assurance. So let us see what we are told here.

People say, 'What do you mean by assurance?' Now this is something that we have already considered, but here we are reminded that there are two great elements in assurance, and the first is the element of a *direct witness*.

The witness of the Spirit

As we have seen, the supreme, the highest form of assurance, comes when men and women enjoy a direct witness, when 'the Spirit itself beareth witness with our spirit, that we are the children of God' (Romans 8:16). This assurance is not based on any deduction; it is the action of the Spirit. We were told of Abel: 'by which he obtained witness that he was righteous, God testifying of his gift' (Hebrews 11:4). And the same was true of Enoch. You remember that 'before his translation he had this testimony, that he pleased God' (v.5). But here we see it, I think, in a very striking manner.

There are some people who seem to confine assurance to the indirect method. They say that you can be assured of your salvation by deducing it from the Scriptures. I agree with that. They say that you can deduce it by what you find in yourself: the graces, and so on. Perfectly right. They say, further, that you can deduce it by the way God treats you, so that when you enjoy blessings you can say, 'I must be a child of God or God would not be dealing with me like this.' But they stop at that and say that you can be assured of your salvation by taking these things together.

But I do want to go on emphasising that there is an assurance altogether higher than that—an immediate assurance that comes when God speaks directly to men and women, giving them an inner certainty, quite apart from any means, that they are his children, and he is their Father. Now that comes out very strikingly here. Look at the position of Abraham. Imagine his feelings when he was given this command to take Isaac and to offer him up as a burnt offering. Imagine his feelings as he went along the road on that journey. Circumstances were altogether against him and it looked as if God was displeased with him. Abraham was not deducing his assurance of salvation from his circumstances, which were calculated to fill him with doubt.

So why was he able to obey God? The answer is that he had direct assurance. He knew, in spite of circumstances. And this is a vital matter. Assurance is such that we still have it whatever may be happening to us. God is still speaking to us; God is still making his presence known to us. Therefore we must emphasise this direct, immediate aspect of assurance.

> *Though all things seem against us*
> *To drive us to despair,*
> *We know one gate is open,*
> *One ear will hear our prayer.*
> Oswald Allen

Or, as another hymn puts it:

> *Though vine nor fig-tree neither*
> *Their wonted fruit should bear,*
> *Though all the field should wither,*
> *Nor flocks nor herds be there . . .*
> William Cowper

It does not matter. In spite of circumstances, an inner witness is given, God's testimony is available to the child of God.

The use of reason

But there is another element that goes with the witness of the Spirit and is equally important. It is seen in the word 'accounting' in the nineteenth verse. We are told that Abraham was able to go ahead, 'accounting [reckoning] that God was able to raise him up, even from the dead; from whence also he received him in a figure'. Now this is where one sees the glory of God's way of salvation and the perfection of all his arrangements. We are not left only with a sensation, a sensibility, an inner consciousness that cannot be put into words and explained or demonstrated. In addition, we are given something external and objective. And the two work together to enable us to go forward.

In other words, Abraham was also able to apply his powers of reason. The devil was there, tempting Abraham and saying: 'What of the promises of God now? What of your claim to be the child of God and the heir of God's great purpose? And what about this Isaac of yours, through whom you say God is going to do all this—what of him now? You are going to put him to death; you are going to offer him as a burnt sacrifice!'

But Abraham was able to account, he was able to reason and argue. He said, in effect, 'Yes, even if this happens, I know that God has the power to raise Isaac up from the dead. I know that nothing is impossible with God.' So Abraham was able to work out what he felt and almost instinctively knew. As the result of this inner witness, he was able to buttress, to confirm and to support his actions, reasoning from all he knew concerning God.

Now it is important that we should bear those two elements in mind; we must not go from one extreme to the other. There are people who are afraid of the direct witness. They are afraid of becoming too subjective. They are afraid of listening to false spirits. Yes, the New Testament knows all about that; that is why it says, 'Believe not every spirit, but try [test] the spirits whether they are of God' (1 John 4:1). But let us be very careful lest, in

71

our fear of the false, we become guilty of quenching the Spirit. In our desire to keep everything orderly and neat, and only in the Word, let us not exclude the activity of the Spirit altogether by forgetting the witness of the Spirit. God speaks by the Spirit *and* the Word; there is a direct work of the Spirit and there is also the work of the Spirit through the Word. And I am suggesting that at this point the story of Abraham demonstrates this truth in a very remarkable manner.

The extent of assurance

The next great principle is the extent to which assurance can go. Now this is strikingly brought out by this particular incident. How far does assurance take me? And here it is remarkably obvious that assurance is always clear and unmistakable. There is no limit to it.

Look at the position of Abraham. Suddenly the command came to take his son, his only son Isaac, and offer him up as a burnt offering, and he immediately set off. On what grounds did he go? There is only one answer: he was absolutely certain that it was God who was telling him to sacrifice his son. Otherwise, he could not possibly have obeyed. Everything that is natural revolts at the very thought; every human argument is against it. The thing is impossible; it is inconsistent. How could God at one and the same time give a son and say, 'This is the one', and then give orders to kill him?

Knowing God's voice

Yet Abraham obeyed. And the only explanation is that he knew, beyond any doubt whatsoever, that it was the voice of God that was speaking to him and commanding him. How could he know that? Again, there is only one answer: his knowledge of God was such that he knew beyond any doubt at all when God was speaking. That is the extent of assurance.

In other words, we are taught here that it is possible, while we are in this life, to have such an intimate knowledge of God that we can be absolutely certain when he speaks to us. Even when his words appear to be the direct opposite of all we had previously understood, we can know him so well, we can be so familiar with his accent, we can be so sure of the tone of his voice, that we can say, 'This is God!'

The devil will come and say, 'Impossible!' Or perhaps our own reason will say to us, 'This is the temptation of the devil.' There is only one answer to that. It is that we so know God that there is no doubt. He may be saying the most impossible thing, judged by human reason; it may be the most ridiculous thing for someone to do; and yet that person gets up and does it. He knows; he is absolutely certain.

I have already quoted the old Puritan's dying testimony: 'Tell them', he said, 'that God dealeth familiarly with men!' It is possible for us so to know God in this way that we are more sure of his voice than of anything else. Assurance can take us as far as that. It is possible for mortal men and women in Christ Jesus, and as children of God, to get so near to their Father that even this is possible.

Do we know anything about this? This is Christianity. This is what we are meant to be as Christians. Oh, that God would deliver us from always judging our Christianity by contrasting ourselves with those who are out in the world, and with the headlines in the newspapers! That is not the way to measure ourselves. How easy it is not to be like the world! No, this is the test: Do we know the voice of God beyond dispute, beyond mistake? Let us be positive, let us examine ourselves in the light of these things. Assurance can go as far as that.

Confidence
Knowing God's voice gives us wonderful confidence. Look at the confidence of Abraham as he goes along that road. Suddenly

Isaac says, 'I can see everything here except the lamb'—'where is the lamb for a burnt offering?' And Abraham says, 'My son, God will provide himself a lamb' (Genesis 22:8). He has no idea how it is to happen. There is nothing to help him. But he knows God, and he says, in effect, 'I know God in such a manner that I know that everything my God orders is right. I do not know how, but I know it is true; it must be, because God is God.'

And notice how the author of Hebrews brings out the extent of Abraham's confidence. 'By faith Abraham, when he was tried, offered up Isaac: and he that had received the promises offered up his only begotten son, of whom it was said, That in Isaac shall thy seed be called.' The whole thing seemed so utterly wrong; God seemed to be going back on his promises and making them ridiculous. Isaac of everybody! The only begotten son, the one in whom the promises were residing—he was to be put to death!

Abraham was able to go on because his certainty gave him confidence. He knew that all would be well, and that, whatever the outcome, God would bring his promise to pass because he would not break his word. Abraham said: God has his own way. I do not know what it is, but I know that God is sure and certain, that his promises never fail.

And, let me remind you again, this was written for our instruction, so that we may have that intimate, certain knowledge of God, and whatever may be happening, may go on with full assurance, with a quiet certainty, nothing doubting. The story of Abraham, I say again, is in many ways the supreme illustration of the assurance of faith and the assurance of salvation. Only someone who knows God and has this relationship to him could conceivably obey God as Abraham obeyed him.

I pause to ask again: Do we possess this kind of assurance? When everything seems to be going wrong, do we rest in peace? Are Paul's words to the Philippians true of us? Are we 'careful [anxious] for nothing' (Philippians 4:6)—nothing at all? If you are asked to offer up your Isaac, can you 'Be careful for nothing'? You should be not only not anxious, but able to help others who are anxious—'Father, where is the lamb?' 'It's all right, my son, God will provide a lamb.'

You are not carrying your own burden only, you are carrying other people's burdens as well, and you are not anxious. 'Be careful for nothing'—everything is included there—'but in every thing by prayer and supplication with thanksgiving let your requests be made known unto God. And the peace of God, which passeth all understanding,'—of course it does! Who can understand a thing like this? Where is your little human reason? You are in another realm altogether—'the peace of God, which passeth all understanding,' descends upon you and garrisons your heart and your mind, and you are at perfect peace though everything is working against you and everything seems to be going wrong.

Assurance is given. It is immediate. It is direct. You are not making deductions here. There is more than that; there is absolute certainty. You say to yourself, 'This is God commanding me, I know it is God!' You cannot give reasons. How easy to imagine the conversation between Abraham and Sarah, and all that Sarah would have to say at such a juncture! It does not matter. Abraham would simply say, 'I know that it is God who has given me this command.' You cannot prove things like this, but you have an absolute inner certainty; your knowledge of God is such, and he makes it so plain and clear, that there is no doubt at all. That is something of the extent of assurance.

And this brings me to my last heading:

The testing of assurance

Again, from the practical standpoint this is most important, and I have no doubt but that the author of the Epistle to the Hebrews added verses 17, 18 and 19 for this very special reason. We are all so liable to misunderstand the question of assurance.

The moment we become Christians, we tend to think like this: 'Now I have become a child of God and have a measure of assurance, everything will go well.' We think that obviously, if we are the chosen children of God, he will smile upon us, and shower his blessings upon us. That is the common assumption.

When trials come

But when things go wrong, people who think like this have a problem. They say, 'Why is this happening to me? This is all wrong. I don't understand it. If God is my Father, why is he treating me as if he were not? Indeed, I see that the ungodly are having a very much better time than I am. Ever since I became a Christian I've had difficulties, but look at those other people . . .' Like the man in Psalm 73, they say, 'For there are no bands in their death: but their strength is firm . . . Their eyes stand out with fatness: they have more than heart could wish' (vv.4,7). What a wonderful life they're having, and here am I: 'I have cleansed my heart in vain' (v.13).

That so often happens. People seem to think that because they are children of God, they should never have any troubles. Of course, evangelism is partly responsible for this. A superficial evangelism can at times be a lying evangelism. It tells people, 'Come to Christ and you will never have another problem. He will solve your problems for you. He will do everything.' Then they find themselves in trouble and ask, 'Is Christianity true?'

But the Bible does not tell us things like that. Indeed, it tells us the exact opposite: 'Whom the Lord loveth he chasteneth,' says the author of Hebrews, 'and scourgeth every son whom he receiveth' (Hebrews 12:6). A great case could be made out for the argument that if there are no troubles in your life, you had better make sure that you are a Christian. God's people are subject to trials and testing. So let us get rid of this notion that because you are a child of God you never have any problems. No, no! Faith—

assurance—is tested. It was tested very severely in the case of Abraham. God tried him—he did not tempt him; we must not use that word. 'God cannot be tempted with evil, neither tempteth he any man' (James 1:13). But he does test us, he does try us. And at the same time we find the value of assurance.

Why trials come

Why, then, did this happen to Abraham? It is obvious that God was not testing Abraham in order to gain information. God knows the end from the beginning. He knows all things; he is omniscient. So why did he do it? And the answer is given quite plainly in Hebrews 11 and 12.

Testing is first and foremost a part of our training, *a preparation for that which God has awaiting us*. That is the great theme, as I say, of the next chapter. 'If ye endure chastening, God dealeth with you as with sons' (v.7). 'Furthermore', says the writer, 'we have had fathers of our flesh which corrected us, and we gave them reverence: shall we not much rather be in subjection unto the Father of spirits, and live? For they verily for a few days chastened us after their own pleasure; but he for our profit, that we might be partakers of his holiness' (vv.9-10).

My dear friends, if you and I only had some conception of the glory to which we are going, and of the holiness of heaven, we would see the need for preparation. Oh, how we need to be cleansed and purified and purged! How we need to have certain edges chiselled off us! We are on our way to glory, we are going to an absolute holiness, and how unready and imperfect we are! God has to teach us more of the way of godliness and of holiness. He is engaged in the great work of preparing his children for that everlasting glory which is God himself. And the moment you take that view, then you see how our faith needs to be tested.

Many of us think we have great faith. Then a test comes and we find we are shaking, we are doubting, and everything seems to collapse. So God tests us in order that we might understand these things. He wants us to know ourselves better. We think we know ourselves, but we do not. We have a wonderful feeling in a meeting and say, 'Never again will I doubt!' But then a little trial comes and we are unsure of everything. We must learn not to rely on feelings or moods; we must not rely only on circumstances. The ancient Greeks had discovered this: 'Know thyself,' they said; that is the great first principle. And the Bible is ever teaching the same thing.

God, by testing us and trying us, gives us *a deeper knowledge of ourselves*, a knowledge that is not only negative but positive. It is wonderful when people react positively to one of these testing trials. They discover that they have more faith than they thought they had. They look back and say, 'You know, I never thought I could go through that!' But they found they could. Why? Because God enabled them. So they learn about themselves, about the value, the power and the strength of faith, what faith can enable them to do. So God, as it were, puts us through these exercises.

The author of Hebrews sums it up like this: 'No chastening for the present seemeth to be joyous, but grievous'—we are all lazy by nature and God puts us into the gymnasium where our muscles are exercised; and they become painful, so that we feel we cannot do any more; but God keeps us working and the muscles are developed—'nevertheless afterward it yieldeth the peaceable fruit of righteousness unto them which are exercised thereby' (Hebrews 12:11). And by putting him to this particular test God was training the muscles of Abraham's faith in order that he might be a man after his own heart.

God trains us all like this in order that we might know ourselves better, but, still more important, he also does it *in order that we might get to know him better*. For every one of us this is the fundamental trouble. We do not know God. We believe things about him, and that is good. But we are not to stop at that. We are not only to believe things about God, we are to know him—and oh, this wonderful knowledge which Abraham had of God! He knew him much better after this incident than he had ever known him before. Everything that happens to you, if you are a child of God, should lead you to this greater knowledge.

It was here that Abraham discovered, more deeply than ever, the purpose of God, the character of God and, above all, the power and might of God. Abraham had been able to reason it out. He had said: 'I know God is able to raise the dead if necessary.' But God showed him that it was not necessary for this to happen, though it could happen. In effect, he said to Abraham, 'You are quite right, Abraham, but because you see it, I need not demonstrate it to you.' So God enlarges our knowledge.

Why is this? I think it must be that God wants to get us into a position in which we will trust him utterly and absolutely in the dark, regardless of what is happening. And Abraham passed that test. Though he did not understand, he said: 'God has asked me, God has commanded me, so I do it.'

And God confirmed to Abraham that he had passed. That is what the angel said to Abraham when he called out to him to stop: 'Lay not thine hand upon the lad, neither do thou anything unto him: for now I know that thou fearest God' (Genesis 22:12)— which means, 'I know that you are always ready to do what I tell you, whatever it is'.

So for us also, whether we understand it or not, we say:

> *Thy way, not mine, O Lord,*
> *However hard it be!*
> Horatius Bonar

We are ready to follow him wherever he may ask us to go, in spite of every single contradiction.

Then a further reason for God's testing of us is, thank God, *that we may have yet greater assurance.*

And the angel of the LORD called unto Abraham out of heaven the second time [he had already called once] and said, By myself have I sworn, saith the LORD, for because thou hast done this thing, and hast not withheld thy son, thine only son: that in blessing I will bless thee, and in multiplying I will multiply thy seed as the stars of the heaven, and as the sand which is upon the sea shore; and thy seed shall possess the gate of his enemies; and in thy seed shall all the nations of the earth be blessed; because thou hast obeyed my voice (Genesis 22:15-18).

God tests the assurance that we may have, in order that he may give us greater assurance—and so it continues. We think we know someone, but then we live with that person and we get to know one another better and better and better. And so it is with God.

The tragedy of the modern Church, it seems to me, is that we all tend to remain at the beginning. Salvation is everything. 'We are saved,' we say. And there we stop. But do you know God better than you knew him a year ago? Are you more certain of God today than you were ten years ago? Is your knowledge of God increasing so that you have a greater confidence and a greater trust? Once you are tested and have passed the test, God will give you a greater knowledge. He speaks the second time, and the third, and the fourth.

Christian people, are we growing in assurance? We are meant to. This notion that we were happiest at the moment we were converted than we ever will be again is a lie; it is unscriptural. But how many Christians there are who say that! They say, 'I haven't got the joy I had at the beginning.' But you should have more, my friend. You should 'grow in grace, and in the knowledge of our Lord and Saviour Jesus Christ' (2 Peter 3:18). You should not remain a babe in Christ; you should become a young person, then middle-aged, then old, increasing in your knowledge of him. 'The angel spake unto Abraham the second time.' It is to increase the assurance.

But lastly, I believe God tested Abraham for this reason—and I say it with reverence and with some hesitation; yet I believe these verses entitle me to say it—God tested Abraham *in order that he might show the whole world what he can make of someone who trusts him and believes him.* Notice this: 'Now they desire a better country, that is, an heavenly: *wherefore God is not ashamed to be called their God:* for he hath prepared for them a city' (Hebrews 11:16). The almighty God has made himself known in this way.

When God called Moses to give him his great task, Moses was a little confused and asked, 'Who are you?' And God said he was 'The LORD God of your fathers, the God of Abraham, the God of Isaac, and the God of Jacob' (Exodus 3:15). In this way he ties himself to us. He made of these men people of whom he could say, 'I am not ashamed to be called their God.' It is as if God is saying, 'You can describe me like this—I am the God of a man like Abraham. I have made him what he is. I am that man's God. I am not like these pagan gods, these deities that do not exist, these idols, these phantoms, these mere projections of people's thoughts. No, no, this is the sort of God I am—the God of Abraham, the God of Isaac, and the God of Jacob.'

And you and I are to be such that God says things like that to us and about us. We read in 2 Corinthians 6:17-18: 'Wherefore come out from among them, and be ye separate, saith the Lord, and touch not the unclean thing; and I will receive you, and I will be a Father unto you, and ye shall be my sons and daughters, saith the Lord Almighty.' So God tested Abraham in order that he might hold him up, as it were, before the world and say, 'I am the God who makes a man like Abraham the man he is.'

And the privilege that is being offered to you and to me is something like this: that God may say to this present generation, and to subsequent generations, 'If you want to know anything about me, I am the God of that man, that woman.' We are to live

81

with such trust and confidence in God, with such intimate knowledge of him, and with such obedience, that God may say to people who do not know him, 'Look at them, and come to me, and I will be your God.'

Yes, this is wonderful! But he has a higher designation of himself. He is 'the God and Father of our Lord and Saviour Jesus Christ', and he is our God because he is his God. I cannot leave this without just holding it before you. Over and above all that we have considered, we have in this story concerning Abraham a prefiguring of something else. Abraham did not actually slay Isaac, but God has smitten and has slain his only begotten Son 'that whosoever believeth in him should not perish, but have everlasting life' (John 3:16). That is the measure of the love of God to us—that he gave his Son for us, as a sweet-smelling savour, as a sacrifice, as an offering. 'He . . . spared not his own Son, but delivered him up for us all' (Romans 8:32).

That is the God in whom we believe—the God of Abraham, and of Isaac, and of Jacob, the God and Father of our Lord and Saviour Jesus Christ. Is he your God? Do you ever think of him as 'my God'? That is what we are called to, we who have the privilege and the right of being called 'the children of God'.

5
Moses:
seeing God

*'But as many as received him, to them gave he power
to become the sons of God, even to them that believe
on his name: which were born, not of blood, nor of the will
of the flesh, nor of the will of man, but of God.'*
(John 1:12-13)

*'By faith Moses, when he was born, was hid
three months of his parents, because they saw he was
a proper child; and they were not afraid of the king's
commandment. By faith Moses, when he was come
to years, refused to be called the son of Pharaoh's daughter;
choosing rather to suffer affliction with the people of God, than
to enjoy the pleasures of sin for a season; esteeming the
reproach of Christ greater riches than the treasures in Egypt:
for he had respect unto the recompence of the reward.
By faith he forsook Egypt, not fearing the wrath of the king:
for he endured, as seeing him who is invisible. Through
faith he kept the passover, and the sprinkling of blood,
lest he that destroyed the firstborn should touch them. By
faith they passed through the Red sea as by dry land:
which the Egyptians assaying to do were drowned.'*
(Hebrews 11:23-29)

We come now to the case of Moses. You will have noticed, as
you have read Hebrews 11, that the two men to whom the

greatest amount of space and attention is given are Abraham and Moses, and that, of course, is not a bit surprising. Abraham was the father of the nation. He is described in the New Testament as the father of the faithful (see Romans 4:11; Galatians 3:7), so it is natural that he should be given prominence.

Moses is of great importance because he was the great law-giver, the one to whom God gave the law that he might give it to the people. So he is a pivotal character in the whole story of the children of Israel. These are the two outstanding men, the men in particular to whom the Israelites always looked back. 'Abraham, our father', and Moses the great lawgiver who had led them out of the captivity of Egypt into the promised land of Canaan.

Now I must impress upon you again this important principle. The writer is not really concerned about the details of these people's lives. He is interested in that which made them what they were, and that was their assurance. This, he tells us, was their whole secret.

Now Hebrews 11 often gets misused because that vital principle has not been borne in mind. Take, for instance, the trial of Abraham, when God called upon him to sacrifice his son Isaac. How often has that been dealt with as an appeal and an exhorta-tion: 'Have you sacrificed your Isaac?' Great pressure is brought upon us to sacrifice our Isaacs, and we are told that if only we will do that, then we shall have a great blessing.

But that is a complete misunderstanding and misuse of this chapter. It is to reverse its meaning. The way in which this chap-ter puts it is this: it was because of their faith and their assurance that these men and women were able to do these things. It was because of his assurance that Abraham was able to offer up Isaac. So you do not start by offering up your Isaac. You must concen-trate on acquiring assurance, on making certain of your faith. The teaching is that if you have the faith of Abraham, if you have his assurance, then if ever you should find yourself called upon to offer your Isaac, you will be able to obey, you will be able to face the test of having to make such an offering. It is tragic that so often people reverse the teaching of this chapter and spend their lives trying to offer up their Isaacs in order that they may get a great blessing.

The story of Moses

Now we have come to Moses, and it is his assurance that we must examine because it was on the ground of this assurance that he was able to do the astounding things that he did. You will find the story in the book of Exodus—one of the greatest stories, not only in the Bible, but in the whole of literature.

The author of Hebrews reminds us that Moses 'refused to be called the son of Pharaoh's daughter'. Now that was how he had been known. You remember how he was born at a time when the edict had gone out that all the male children born to the Hebrews were to be put to death. So when this little child was born, he 'was hid for three months of his parents, because they saw he was a proper child' (v.23), which means that he was very beautiful. As they looked at this newborn baby, his parents knew that they could not possibly put him to death. So they hid him, you remember, among the reeds and the rushes in the river, and there he was discovered by Pharaoh's daughter. And though she sent him to his own mother to be brought up, she regarded him as her own son, and so did Pharaoh and everybody else. She adopted him and gave him all the privileges and all the wonderful prospects of a prince of Egypt. There was never a man who had a more shining and glorious career ahead of him than this man Moses.

But we are told that all this changed 'when he was come to years'—that is, 'when he was full forty years old' (Acts 7:23). For forty years Moses had enjoyed all the privileges of the palace with the attendant power and future prospects. Then he suddenly renounced it all. He made the great decision that he would no longer be known as the son of Pharaoh's daughter.

Moses decided to identify himself with people who were nothing but slaves, people in abject suffering. That is what verse 25 means: he laid aside all that belonged to him, and became one with these Hebrew slaves. And in addition to that, he even risked his life. He found an Egyptian abusing one of his own fellow countrymen, and decided he must do something about it. So he slew the Egyptian and buried him in the sand. But unfortunately this was observed and so Moses had to flee for his life.

The point I am emphasising is that Moses not only gave up his great position but even risked his life, and became a shepherd in the land of Midian. It is very difficult for us to take this in: how a man accustomed to the learning and the pomp and the show of the palace of Pharaoh, should suddenly become just a humble shepherd looking after a flock of sheep, moving them from one pasture to another, a mere nobody in a foreign land. It is remarkable that he should have humbled himself to that extent.

But—and I want to emphasise this because it is something that we do not always realise—Moses decided to leave that happy life of a shepherd. I call it a happy life, because it was a life of safety and of comparative ease, a life which did not involve him in any trouble. The life of a shepherd is a simple life. But this man left all that and took upon himself, at the behest of God, a life that was to be full of risks and dangers, a life demanding constant thought and meditation in response to most difficult and involved problems.

Now I emphasise this because sometimes it is more difficult to give up a life of ease than it is to give up a great position. It depends upon your temperament, of course, but these two types of person are in most of us. The greatness and the pomp may appeal to us, but then we may be lazy also, and we say, 'Anything for a quiet life.' You have given up one life and have taken up a second, and have decided that this will suit you for the rest of your life, because, after all, it is much better. It is an easier life than the life of the palace, and you are not involved in high decision-making. You can just go on looking after the sheep and meditating, and writing poetry if you feel so disposed—what a wonderful life this is! Not the life of a city, but the quiet life of the country.

But suddenly the call comes, 'Get out of that!' And the decision to obey can be much more difficult than the first decision. But Moses responded to that also. He entered into one of the most difficult and involved and trying lives that a man has ever lived.

Next, we see Moses defying the great Pharaoh. He had risked his life by going back at all, but he did not stop at that. He spoke to Pharaoh; he stood up to him and defied him, uttering the message of God without any fear whatsoever. And he was a meek man, the meekest man of all, the Bible tells us (Numbers 12:3). The record makes it quite clear that he was a naturally nervous man, a man who was diffident, lacking self-confidence. But he stood boldly before this mighty Pharaoh, 'not fearing the wrath of the king' (Hebrews 11:27). What boldness!

Not only that. Moses kept the Passover, killed the lambs, and painted the blood on the doorposts and the lintels. Then he marched the Hebrew people out of Egypt, though he knew that they would be followed by the hosts and the chariots of Pharaoh. And what is still more amazing is that not merely did he defy the might and power of a Pharaoh and all his hosts, but that he was able to do it with the mob that he was leading, with the children of Israel, who were always ready to grumble and to complain, always wanting to be turning back, always losing hope and whimpering and crying—oh, the fickleness of the children of Israel! And Moses led them out in spite of these two difficulties.

And finally, Moses led the people through the Red Sea. 'By faith they passed through the Red sea as by dry land' (v.29). That, I think, is the most dramatic incident in the whole of the Bible. And it was the faith of Moses, not of the children of Israel, that

87

took them to safety. Moses had led the people out, and suddenly they found themselves trapped: a mountain on one side—Pi-hahiroth; a mountain on the other side—Baal-zephon (Exodus 14:2); the Red Sea in front of them; and behind, Pharaoh and his army. What could they do? They were absolutely hemmed in. Impossible! But it was at that tremendous moment that Moses was able to obey the command of the Lord. God said, 'Speak unto the children of Israel, that they go forward' (Exodus 14:15), and he gave the command and on they went through the Red Sea.

The motivating force

There, then, is a list of the things that this man Moses did. The writer of the letter to the Hebrews reminds us of these details. But now let us follow his method and see why he gives us these facts about Moses. I have told you of what Moses did, but now let me ask this question: What was it that made him do all this? And we are given the answer here in a very interesting and most important manner, and this is the essential teaching of this whole chapter.

Moses did not do these things as the result of obeying an intuition, or because he had some odd feeling or instinct; he did not follow some sort of hunch when he plunged into action. No, no, that is not Christianity. Moses did all this as the result of a very definite process, a process which is summed up here in two vital words in verses 25 and 26.

The first word is *choosing*: 'Choosing rather to suffer affliction with the people of God, than to enjoy the pleasures of sin for a season.' The second word is *esteeming*: 'Esteeming the reproach of Christ greater riches than the treasures in Egypt.' The apostle Paul uses the same word exactly in Philippians 3:7-8, where he says, 'What things were gain to me, those I *counted* loss for Christ. Yea doubtless, and I *count* all things but loss . . .' He, too, was esteeming; he was working it out.

Choosing

There are two great principles here, and this is important because it gives us a valuable test that we can all apply to ourselves. First, the Christian is always in the position of considering two alternatives. When I say two alternatives, I am, of course, speaking in an ultimate sense. I am not referring to the small daily choices we all have to make. But I mean that two big possibilities are always before the Christian—and only the Christian.

Those who are not Christians do not know anything about this. They only know one thing: the worldly view of life. Of course, there are many possibilities in that life. There may be problems over which car or which house to buy. It all belongs to the realm of this world. But Christians see two ways, they are looking at two possibilities: a 'strait' gate or a wide gate; a narrow way or a broad way; a way that leads to life or a way that leads to destruction; a spiritual way or a carnal, earthly, worldly way. Christian men and women are always aware of these two great, total possibilities before them, which cover the whole of their lives and their every activity.

You see, therefore, that Moses was constantly face to face with the two alternatives: the son of Pharaoh's daughter or life with the people of God; remaining as a shepherd in the wilderness or obeying the call of God. And this involved him in a total decision. The whole man and all his circumstances were involved. And this, I say again, is true of every Christian. Christians are always facing these two calls, these two options: God and the devil; heaven and hell; the spiritual life and the worldly life. They are aware of this, and they always have to choose.

Esteeming

The next principle is that Christians always evaluate everything in the light of the gospel. That is their standard. That was Moses' secret. He did not, I repeat, act from an intuition or on impulse.

89

When he slew the Egyptian who was maltreating his fellow countryman, it was not a sudden spasm, as it were, but the end of a long process. He had been working it out and the hour had come to strike.

This revelation of God given in the gospel enables Christians, first, to *see through the world*. They have a test that they can apply to everything and it comes out like this: 'Choosing rather to suffer affliction with the people of God, than to enjoy the pleasures of sin for a season' (v.25).

So when Moses looked at the life of the palace, all the pomp and ceremony surrounding a Pharaoh, and his own future as a prince in Egypt, he did not only see that. He immediately put it into the light and the context of the revelation of God concerning God himself, and humanity, and life, and God's glory. And what had at one time appeared so attractive became sin. To live for that, to make that his life, became sinful; it meant going against the call of God. His own conscience, and everything within him, condemned it.

Moses had the great insight to see that the pleasures of Egypt were only 'for a season'. The whole trouble in the world is that men and women do not realise that. People say, 'Isn't life wonderful! I'm enjoying myself. I've never had it so good. I'm drinking and eating more than ever. I've a better car than I've ever had! Religion? Nonsense! Rubbish!'

Those are 'the pleasures of sin for a season', but people do not stop to see that; they do not know it. Why not? It is because they are not Christians. Christians have this other view, this higher understanding, and they know that all those things will vanish, that although a man may be a Pharaoh, he must die and crumble into dust in the grave. The Christian sees through it all. 'This is the victory that overcometh the world, even our faith' (1 John 5:4).

Secondly, the gospel gives Christians *a positive understanding of the Christian life*. The two always go together: you see through this world; you also see God's kingdom and God's purposes. And Moses was able to see exactly the meaning of suffering: 'Choosing rather to suffer affliction with the people of God . . . esteeming the reproach of Christ greater riches than the treasures of Egypt.' That is a tremendous statement. It means something like this: Moses was able to look upon suffering in this life in an entirely new manner. In effect, he said, 'If I obey God, it will involve me in the reproach and suffering which is inherent in the life of God's people, but it is all right, I can see that there is value in that.'

Moses saw that 'whom the Lord loveth he chasteneth, and scourgeth every son whom he receiveth' (Hebrews 12:6). He could see a healing value in suffering. So when trials and troubles came, he did not just lie down on the ground and grumble and complain as the children of Israel so often did. No, no, he had a higher understanding and said: 'All this is the result of sin and the fall. This is not God but the devil. But God, through it all and beyond it all, has a great purpose with respect to me. He can even use that for my good.'

'I have learned, in whatsoever state I am, therewith to be content,' says the apostle Paul in Philippians 4:11. And Moses had discovered the same secret.

But, thirdly, there is even *a privilege in suffering.* 'Esteeming the reproach of Christ greater riches than the treasures in Egypt.' Now this term 'the reproach of Christ' means that we are treading in the steps of Christ who has gone before us. If ever a man suffered reproach in this world it was the Son of God when he became man. 'He is despised and rejected of men' (Isaiah 53:3)— that is the summing up. He suffered reproach and ignominy. And Christians are men and women who see that they have the great and high privilege of being like their Master. So the apostle Peter makes a great appeal to us when we are despised and insulted. He says: Be like him. 'Follow his steps . . . who, when he was reviled,

91

reviled not again; when he suffered, he threatened not; but committed himself to him that judgeth righteously' (1 Peter 2:21,23).

The apostle Paul teaches exactly the same thing. He says: Do not grumble and complain when you find yourself in trouble. 'For unto you it is given in the behalf of Christ, not only to believe on him, but also to suffer for his sake' (Philippians 1:29). It is a high privilege! 'My brethren, count it all joy', says James, 'when ye fall into divers temptations' (James 1:2). So Christian men and women say, 'I will do that. I'm not going to be troubled by the reproach. I'm walking in the line. I'm following him—the reproach of Christ!' They regard suffering for Christ as the highest honour.

And so we find that some of the early Christians, when they were finally face to face with martyrdom and were being thrown to the lions in the arena, thanked God that at last they had been accounted worthy to suffer shame for his name's sake. The early Christians used to say that the final crown of glory that a Christian was allowed to wear was martyrdom. Death for Christ was a crown. As the athlete who won the contest was crowned, here was the final crown of glory—martyrdom! The reproach of Christ!

Now those were the considerations that operated in the case of Moses. We have seen the things that he did, yes, but this is the important question: What made him do it? And there is the answer. He saw the two ways. He saw the glory of this way, and the other became sinful to him. So he obeyed God and went forward.

The enabling power

But there is another principle which is the most important of all. We have seen what made Moses act as he did—the choosing and the esteeming. Yes, but what enabled him? It is one thing to see these things theoretically, but here is a man who acted on what he saw. What was the secret?

The answer is vital: it is *assurance*. Here we see the difference between an intellectual assent to the truth and living by the truth. The only thing that can ever enable you to live as Moses lived is assurance. 'Faith is the substance of [the] things hoped for, the evidence of things not seen' (11:1). There was no uncertainty. That is why Moses was able actually to do what he did. You do not start by trying to imitate Moses. No, no, you must acquire his assurance. So let us look at that.

The source of assurance

How did Moses get his assurance? This, again, is a most impor-tant question, and the records make it fairly plain and clear to us. I have no doubt that he got it at the beginning from his own mother. His father and mother are included in the list of those who had faith: 'By faith Moses, when he was born, was hid three months of his parents'—that is the faith of Amram and Jochebed, his parents—'because they saw he was a proper child; and they were not afraid of the king's commandment' (v.23).

And it seems quite clear that as Moses' parents brought him up, they told him who he was and why they had acted as they did. They told him the great secret of the children of Israel. They were slaves for the moment in Egypt—it did not matter, they knew the story. Every Israelite was taught it, and Jochebed taught it to Moses. So though he was called the son of Pharaoh's daughter, Moses knew this other story. It was always with him.

I do not know, but it is not difficult to speculate that there was something else. Over and above this, God was speaking to Moses. As he grew up and became a young man, God began to deal with him in a more direct manner. We are not told that, but it is inevitable, it seems to me, from the whole teaching of the Bible.

But let me come to something about which we are absolutely certain—the burning bush! There he was, one afternoon, just taking the sheep round to 'the backside of the desert' (Exodus 3:1) to the mountain. He had probably done this many times before. He was not expecting anything; he had settled down into the life of a simple shepherd; but suddenly he beheld a bush that was burning but was not consumed.

Moses was on the point of examining this great mystery, when the voice came to him out of the burning bush, the voice of God. And God spoke to him. And he knew it was God. That was assurance! That was not believing theoretically in God somewhere in the heavens, it was God addressing him: 'Put off thy shoes from off thy feet' (Exodus 3:5). Stand back! He was in the presence of God, hearing the voice of God! That gives assurance; that gives certainty; there is immediacy there. That is not deduction from Scripture—there were no Scriptures. God was speaking to him directly, manifesting himself, proceeding to give him the covenant, and telling him what he proposed to do.

And as we read the story, we find that God spoke to Moses on many other occasions. It was to Moses in particular that God revealed his great name: I AM THAT I AM. He had not given it in that specific manner before. He had used it, but it was through Moses that he gave his great covenant name to the children of Israel. And he stated the terms of the covenant and opened before them what he was going to do. This gives assurance!

Now it is only as you understand this that you see how Moses was able to do what he did. How easy it is for us to read the story of Moses entering into the presence of Pharaoh! And, of course, we all tend to think that we would do the same thing. But you try to imagine it! Imagine yourself standing up in utter helplessness, with just a crowd of helpless, hopeless people behind you, and defying the might of a Pharaoh, and leading out the people! Imagine yourself with Pi-hahiroth and Baal-zephon, and the hosts of Pharaoh, and the Red Sea! How easy it is to read these things, but can you see yourself doing them? What enables someone to do things like that? Well, there is only one answer—

it is absolute assurance; and God had given Moses that assurance in the ways that we have considered. And God had also given him miraculous power, he had enabled him to do things that are supernatural, and it is in the light of all this that Moses obtained his assurance.

The focus of assurance

But let me ask a second question: What was Moses sure of? Because these are the things of which we, too, must be sure.

First, he was sure of *God's purpose and plan of salvation*. He was sure that God was preparing a people for himself out of the world. He had inherited this tradition. His mother had told him of the division, the dividing line that runs right down history: Abel and Cain; God's man, the world's man; Noah and his family, the people of God, the start of a new race, as it were.

And Moses believed all this. He knew about Abraham, Isaac, Jacob—the people of God being prepared, and God's way of salvation. He believed this and was sure of it. He did not take the world as it is, but said, in effect, 'Yes, I know. I see everything as everybody else sees it, but I know that God has a plan. He is calling out a people for himself. He is preparing for the kingdom. He is going on with his plan in spite of what I see.'

Moses was also sure that *the people of Israel were God's people, and he was one of them.* He was a child of God. That is at the back of his great decision not to be called any longer the son of Pharaoh's daughter. So when he saw the Egyptian tyrant maltreating the Hebrew slave, the great moment arrived, and he did not hesitate. He said: These are the people to whom I belong, and this slave is one of God's people. I am regarded as one who belongs to the Egyptians, but I do not. I belong to the people of Israel and I am going to show it!

Then Moses was certain that *he was called to fulfil a special function with respect to God's people.* Thank God that we are told

95

in the records that now and again he hesitated and faltered a little. We are not perfect in this life. But of this he was certain: that God was calling him. He said to God: 'I cannot speak, why are you calling me? I have no power, how can I do it?' 'It is all right,' said God. 'I will be with you. Go on.'

And on Moses went. He was certain that God had called him to lead the people out of captivity into the freedom and the enjoyment of the land flowing with milk and honey. It is a great thing when men and women know that they are called to fulfil a special function in the kingdom of God. In spite of his own meekness and modesty and hesitation, Moses knew that God had called him, and so he persevered.

And Moses was sure of *the coming of Christ*. Notice that the word 'Christ' is used in verse 26: 'the reproach of Christ'. You may ask how those words could be used of Moses, who lived fourteen hundred years before Christ. And the answer is given quite clearly in the Scriptures. We have already seen that Abraham saw the day of Christ, and the same is true of Moses. God had given a revelation to Moses concerning the coming of his Son as the Deliverer. He had not seen it plainly, he had seen it afar off, but he had seen it. This is what he said to the people towards the end of his life: 'The LORD thy God will raise up unto thee a Prophet from the midst of thee, of thy brethren, like unto me; unto him ye shall hearken' (Deuteronomy 18:15). And Stephen, when he was on trial, quoted that, and said that Moses gave that prophecy concerning the coming of the Christ, the Son of God (Acts 7:37). Moses knew that he was suffering the reproach of the Christ of God who was to come.

Moses was sure that *deliverance comes through the shedding of blood*. We are told that 'Through faith he kept the passover, and the sprinkling of blood' (v.28). Now that is not merely something mechanical. He did what he was told to do, yes, but he saw the ultimate meaning—again, not plainly, but he saw it. God always delivers by blood. As we have seen, Abel had understood that when he offered a blood sacrifice, and not the fruit of the ground. 'Without shedding of blood is no remission [of sins],' wrote the author of Hebrews (Hebrews 9:22).

Moses was the man who was given the detailed instructions about the shedding of blood and the burnt offerings and the sacrifices, and the Passover, the blood that covers, the blood that saves, the blood that redeems! The paschal lamb was the foreshadowing of the 'Lamb of God which taketh away the sin of the world' (John 1:29). The whole point made by this writer of the letter to the Hebrews is that Moses was not trying to justify himself by works. He was not saying, 'If I live a good life, I will please God.' No, no! He did not believe it vaguely, but was absolutely sure that Christ's blood would be shed, and it was only in Christ that he and all others could be saved.

And then, of course, Moses was certain of *the ultimate destiny of all God's people*. 'Esteeming the reproach of Christ greater riches than the treasures in Egypt: for he had respect unto *the recompence of the reward.*' That is heaven, my friends. And the men and women whom God can use and who are able to do these exploits in this world, are those who are certain of heaven; they know where they are going. Therefore they are not afraid of tyrants, Pharaohs and all the hosts of the world. They know that 'there remaineth therefore a rest to the people of God' (Hebrews 4:9). This is not an earthly Canaan, though that is included, but a heavenly Canaan beyond it, 'a city which hath foundations, whose builder and maker is God' (v.10).

But the last and the most wonderful thing of all is this: Moses was certain of *God*. 'By faith he forsook Egypt, not fearing the wrath of the king'—why not? What was the secret? 'For he endured'—he kept on—'as seeing him who is invisible.' Moses knew God. He knew the character of God, that God is truth, that God is holy, that God is omnipotent, that his promises are ever

97

sure. 'No man hath seen God at any time' (John 1:18), but Moses knew him, not only the theophany in the burning bush, but he had met him, he had spoken to him, he had access into his holy presence.

One of the greatest chapters in the Old Testament is Exodus 33 where Moses is praying to God and pleading with him. 'Go up,' says God, 'I will send an angel to lead your people into Canaan.' 'No, no,' says Moses, 'we will not go unless you come with us.' 'But I am going to send an angel, and I will give you power.' 'No', says Moses, 'If thy presence go not with me, carry us not up hence' (Exodus 33:15)—do not send us up unless you come with us.

And so Moses pleaded with God. He was a man who knew God. He knew the way into his presence. And he asked God to reveal his glory to him. That was his great concern. He did not merely want to go into Canaan, he wanted to be with God. That is what mattered to him: not the mere possession of a land, but God with them, and God among them, and God blessing them. He saw 'him who is invisible' (v.27)

And so when Moses found himself confronted by the Red Sea, what did he do? The miserable children of Israel were saying, 'Hast thou taken us away to die in the wilderness?' (Exodus 14:11)—Have you brought us up to slaughter us at this point? Why did you ever bring us up? Why don't you take us back?

But Moses cried out to God (Exodus 14:15). He always knew that the way was open. He always knew that God was ready to receive him. 'He endured as seeing him who is invisible.' This is the whole secret of the Christian life: to know God; not merely to believe about God, but to know him.

Full assurance

And this is the whole argument of the author of Hebrews. These men, he says, were all enabled to do the things they did because they knew God. But they belonged to the old dispensation. They had not received the promises, but only saw them afar off, and as we have seen, if it is possible for an Old Testament saint to have this degree of assurance, how much more possible is it for us now! The author contrasts and compares the old dispensation and the new in chapters 8 and 12 of this great epistle. All along he is proving the superiority of the new, because the Son of God has now come and the death on the cross has taken place. How much greater, he says, is our position!

Be careful lest you put the saints of the Old Testament in a higher position than the saints of the New. You say, 'If God appeared to me in a burning bush, then of course I would be able to act as Moses did. If only I had the external assurance that was given to him!' But that is a very wrong and unscriptural argument. What is offered in the New Testament is superior to that which is offered in the Old, and the assurance that you and I should enjoy in Christ and as the result of the outpouring of the Spirit of God on the day of Pentecost—the baptism of the Spirit—should put us in an infinitely higher position.

When you look at these people, great as they were, and put them by the side of a man like the apostle Paul, I say they seem small. Why? Because the apostle was able to look back on Calvary, he was 'in Christ', he had been baptised by the Spirit. 'I know whom I have believed,' he wrote to Timothy (2 Timothy 1:12). This is not a vague, uncertain faith; it is not hoping against hope; it is not trying to hold on as best you can. No, no! 'I know whom I have believed, and am persuaded [certain] that he is able to keep that which I have committed unto him against that day.' There is no doubt about it. 'I know!' 'I am certain!' 'I am persuaded!' 'For to me to live is Christ, and to die is gain' (Philippians 1:21). Paul had absolute certainty. God 'dealing familiarly with men'.

My dear friends, I leave you with this question: Are you living a life 'as seeing him who is invisible'? Is God real to you? Is the

Lord Jesus Christ real to you? That is the New Testament teaching. We are meant to know God. We are meant to know that we are the children of God. We are meant to know ourselves in the presence of God, to have access to God beyond any doubt or uncertainty or any question. 'He endured, as seeing him who is invisible.' Moses walked with God. That is the thing to seek.

We have no right to rest on any position which is less than a full assurance of faith, a full assurance of knowledge, and a full assurance of hope. And as we have this glorious certainty, whatever we may be called upon to face or to do, we shall be enabled to do in precisely the same way as Moses in his day and generation. Give yourselves no rest until you, too, see him who is invisible, and know that God is your God and that you are his child, destined to receive 'the recompence of the reward'.